I0165704

Comforting Job

And All Who Suffer

Robert J. Koester

GWA
Books

COMFORTING JOB
AND ALL WHO SUFFER

© 2024 Robert J. Koester
Cover Design: Pamela Clemons

Unless otherwise indicated, all Scripture quotations from Bible books other than the book of Job are from The ESV® Bible (The Holy Bible, English Standard Version®), copyright © 2001 by Crossway, a publishing ministry of Good News Publishers. Used by permission. All rights reserved.

Unless otherwise indicated, Scripture quotations from the Bible book of Job are from the Holy Bible, Evangelical Heritage Version ® (EHV ®) © 2017 Wartburg Project, Inc. All rights reserved. Used by permission. "EHV" and "Evangelical Heritage Version" are registered trademarks of Wartburg Project, Inc.

All rights reserved. No part of this book may be reproduced or transmitted in any form without the prior written permission of the publisher. Contact the publisher for permission to reprint or to use excerpts beyond fair use.

GWA Books
gwabooks@midco.net
6-25-1
ISBN: 9781734431988
Library of Congress Contol Number: 2024919131

Table of Contents

Introduction v

Part One: Guidelines

Chapter 1—Job Glorified God—Job 1 1

Special Topic: Old Testament Faith

Chapter 2—Job Glorified God Again—Job 2 15

Special Topic: Who Sends Suffering?

Chapter 3—God Vindicated Job—Job 42 25

Special Topic: Job's Perseverance; Christian
Perseverance

Chapter 4—Summary of the Guidelines For
Interpreting Job 43

Special Topic: Why Do People Suffer? Answers from
Scripture

Part Two: The Conversation

Chapter 5—The Conversation, Part One—Job 3–8 71

Special Topic: The Search for Wisdom to Comfort the Suffering

Chapter 6—The Conversation, Part One Continued— Job 9–14.. 103

Special Topic: The Themes in the Conversation

Chapter 7—The Conversation, Part Two—Job 15–21... 139

Special Topic: God Is Just

Chapter 8—The Conversation, Part Three—Job 22–26. 175

Special Topic: Job's Gospel Hope

Chapter 9—Job's Final Words—Job 27–31.................. 199

Special Topic: Can Christians Appeal to Their Own Righteousness Without Being Work-Righteous?

Chapter 10—Elihu Counseled Job—Job 32–37............ 225

Special Topic: Was God Chastening Job?

Chapter 11—God Rebuked Job—Job 38–41 259

Special Topic: God's Wisdom and Power

Chapter 12—Comforting Job 273

Appendix... 297

Scripture Index 303

Introduction

People from all backgrounds are at least a little familiar with Job. Some say, "Why, Job is the man who suffered," Others say, "He was a brave man. He refused to let suffering get him down. He's an inspiration to all of us."

Christians go deeper. Job's example helps them hold on to their confidence in God's forgiveness, grace, and love.

But sometimes, even Christians have a hard time going beyond the basic outline of Job's story. Many know what happened in the first two chapters—how Job's suffering began. They also know that God restored Job's blessings, as revealed in the last chapter. And they know that somewhere in the book Job says, "I know that my Redeemer lives." But the long middle section of the book, which contains the discussion between Job and his friends, and the chapters spoken by Elihu, are little known to all but the most serious Bible readers. I pray that this book will fill whatever blanks remain in your understanding of the book of Job.

In general, each chapter of this book is divided into three sections.

The *first* section, "Getting Into the Book," is a short paraphrase of one or more chapters of the book of Job. Its purpose is to help you see the key thoughts in each chapter. Use it as you wish. You might want to read the

chapters of the book of Job covered in the paraphrase
and then use the paraphrase to better understand what
you just read. Or you might read the paraphrase first
and then read the chapters in Scripture. Or you might
read just the paraphrase in order to move through this
book more quickly.

The *second* section. "Looking at Job," includes comments
on the chapters of Job you just read. It will help you get
the big picture of Job and the points made in the discussion. This section will not go into every verse in detail.
For that, please refer to a commentary on the book of
Job. Rather, it will expand on the paraphrase found in
the first section and go into much more detail on the
points made in the conversation.

All but the last chapter contain a *third* section that
treats a "Special Topic." The special topics are of a more
general nature and go into more detail on key teachings
or questions found in the book.

The present book is divided into *two parts*, which cor-
respond to the parts of Job written in either prose or
poetry. The first two chapters of Job and the last are
written in prose. They tell the story of Job. The first two
chapters talk about the events that took place before
Job's friends arrived. The last chapter, chapter 42, relates
the ways God restored and blessed Job after his time of
suffering.

In part one, we'll search these three chapters to find
"guideposts" to help us understand the book. The first
two chapters give us knowledge of what went on behind
the scenes leading up to Job's suffering. The final chapter
shows how God vindicated Job's faith and restored his

blessings. These guideposts will keep us on track so we don't stray from the purpose of the book or from the lessons found in it.

With the guideposts in hand, in part two we will move into the conversation itself. The bulk of the book of Job is a conversation between Job and his friends. They speak to each other in poetry. In general, these chapters are not as easily understood as the chapters written in prose. Job and his friends make their points with figurative language, illustrations, and long descriptions of God. A simple point may be made quickly in a verse or two or spread out over many lines, often building to a climax.

One thought is sometimes followed by another without an indication that the speaker is moving to a new point. Sometimes the speaker is talking to a person and then begins talking to God. We will want to be aware of when that happens.

Other factors add to the difficulty of interpreting the book of Job. It is uncertain who wrote it or when it was written. If we accept the idea that Solomon wrote Job, we can conclude that Job is another book in which Solomon is sharing his wisdom.

The people in Job are not Israelites, nor does Job find a place in the history of Israel. Job himself is somewhat isolated from the rest of Scripture. In the rest of Scripture, we find only two references to him. By contrast, Abraham is referred to throughout Scripture, especially in the New Testament. We can conclude many things about Abraham by listening to New Testament writers describe his faith and his place in the history of God's promise. But in Job's case we don't have that luxury. Aside from the two other places in Scripture where he is mentioned—which are certainly important—we must depend on the book of Job itself to provide the background information we need to interpret it.

Therefore, we are consigned to interpret the book using the guideposts we find in the book itself, which we will isolate in part one. With this in mind, we will strive to observe the following principles:

Scripture always interprets Scripture. But we dare not use other places in Scripture to interpret the book of Job unless the clear passages of Job open the door for us to do so.

In addition to this, interpreters sometimes determine the meaning of Job on the basis of passages that are open to interpretation. This is especially true in Elihu's case. For example, there are various ways people interpret his attitude. One interpreter might be quite harsh toward Elihu, accusing him of pride and lovelessness. Another interpreter will see Elihu as the ideal pastor for Job, zealous for the truth and eager to help Job live rightly before God. Both opinions are based on interpretations of the same words. We will attempt to let the clearly taught guideposts direct our interpretation.

That said, the book of Job *does* invite speculation, and everyone engages in it. However, if speculation has a major impact on the interpretation of the book, we must always ask if that speculation is consistent with the clear guideposts found in the historical chapters. In this book, if we offer speculation, it will be labelled as such and shown to be consistent with the guideposts we have identified in the prose sections of the book.

In this book, when we quote from the book of Job, we will use the Evangelical Heritage Version's (EHV) translation. For quotations from all other parts of the Bible we will quote from the English Standard Version (ESV).

In the second part of each chapter, the "Looking at Job" section, there will be short citations at the end of some paragraphs that look like this: (1:1,2). This means that the above comments were on Job chapters 1, verses 1 and 2. This will help you keep track of where you are in the chapter. Don't confuse these references with actual quotations, which always include the book of the Bible from where the quotation is taken. All direct quotations from Scripture are cited, for example (Job 1:1,2), and put in quotation marks. But sometimes I want to offer a hypothetical quotation or a short paraphrase of the text. In that case, quotation marks are used, but no Scripture reference is given.

May the Lord bless your study!

Part One: Guidelines

Chapter 1—Job Glorified God—Job 1............................1

Special Topic: Old Testament Faith

Chapter 2—Job Glorified God Again—Job 2.................15

Special Topic: Who Sends Suffering?

Chapter 3—God Vindicated Job—Job 42 25

Special Topic: Job's Perseverance; Christian
Perseverance

**Chapter 4—Summary of the Guidelines For
Interpreting Job** 43

Special Topic: Why Do People Suffer? Answers from
Scripture

Job Glorified God—Job 1

Getting Into the Book

Reading—Chapter 1

Job 1 Job's first trial

Verses 1-3

> There was a man named Job. He was blameless and upright. He loved and served the Lord in everything he did, and he kept himself from whatever displeased the Lord. He had ten children, a large number of possessions, and many servants.

Verses 4,5

> Job knew God forgave his sins. He also wanted God to forgive any sins his children might have committed, especially when they held feasts in their homes. His greatest fear was that they might have cursed God secretly in their hearts. So after their feasts, he offered sacrifices for each of them.

Verses 6–12

> On one occasion, Satan came before God. God pointed out Job as an example of a person who truly respected, loved, and served him. Satan claimed that Job loved God because of all the gifts God had given him. Satan told God to take away Job's blessings and he would see that Job loved God only because of the material blessings God had given him. God then gave Satan control of Job's possessions, to do with them whatever he wished. But he told Satan not to harm Job's body.

Verses 13–19

> In one day, God took away all the blessings he had given Job.

Verses 20–22

> Job expressed grief over his losses, but he did not reject God. In fact, he praised God for giving him everything he had and he acknowledged God's right to take them away. Job did not charge God with wrongdoing.

Looking at Job

Important questions to keep in mind

As we will see, the book of Job is about the search for wisdom to understand the relationship between God and the suffering his people endure. If we can uncover this wisdom, we will be better prepared to comfort others who are suffering.

We find this wisdom as we explore the topics found in Job and answer the questions that arise. We will define and divide these topics in more detail as we continue. But for now, we will distill them down into four general topics and the questions that arise when we consider them.

The first topic is about the reason why Job suffered. As we will see, three of Job's friends came to comfort him. All three explained Job's suffering in the same way: Job was committing great sins, and God was using suffering to prompt Job to give them up. Later, a younger man named Elihu offered an alternate reason for Job's suffering. He explained that God was graciously chastening Job, lovingly trying to get Job to repent of the sins he was committing. Job, on the other hand, did not have a clear answer. Why was he suffering so horribly, he asked? He was a child and servant of God and an innocent person who had always enjoyed God's favor. Throughout Job's part of the conversation, he fluctuated between humble trust in God's ways and accusing God of injustice. If we understand why Job acted like this, we will better understand how to help the suffering people in our lives who are acting in the same way.

The second topic is about the relationship between God, who is perfectly holy, and the evil associated with suffering. Suffering was not in the perfect world God created. It entered the world after Adam and Eve fell into sin. Satan, who is suffering for his sin of rebellion against God, is pleased when God's creatures reject God and suffer along with him. Who, then, was responsible for Job's suffering? for suffering today? Is it Satan, who tries to destroy the faith of God's people, often through the use of suffering? Or is it God, who hates evil but controls everything that happens? The people in the book of Job didn't have as much trouble with this matter as people do today. How we answer that question will determine what we say about God to the sufferers we ourselves are called on to comfort.

The third topic revolves around Job's claim to be righteous. When his friends told Job that he was suffering for his sin, Job said they were wrong and appealed to the fact that he had lived an upright life. What's more, when Job spoke to God, he often reminded God of his blameless life and that he did not deserve to suffer. Was Job right to appeal to his blameless life? Was he correct to base his complaints against his friends and against God on the life he lived prior to his suffering? How we answer that will determine how we judge much of what Job says. And it will help us understand how we should react to similar claims made by the people we are called on to comfort.

The fourth topic is related to all the above. The topic is God's justice. Was God just to cause Job to suffer as he did? Or was God acting unjustly? Some of those we comfort might accuse God of acting unjustly. How should we respond? A related topic is that God's wisdom and power are unlimited. How should those who are in the midst of suffering apply this fact? Should it make them wonder why God is treating them as he is and make them afraid of him? Or should it lead them to trust in him?

In the first part of this book—chapters 1–4—we will find guideposts from the book of Job that will help us think about these topics and answer the questions related to them. They will help us understand the book as a whole and learn how to better comfort the Jobs that come into our lives.

The book begins with a description of Job

The opening verses of chapter 1 give us a striking description of Job's character. One looks in vain for another believer in Scripture who is described in such glowing terms. Because Job's character plays such a central role in the conversation between Job and his friends and in Elihu's words to Job, these verses can be viewed as an introduction to the entire book.

We know little about Job's history. We are told he was from the land of Uz, possibly located east of the Dead Sea in the territory later called Edom.

On the other hand, we are told much about the way Job lived. He was blameless and upright. The Hebrew word here translated "blameless" means "perfect" or "complete." There was no part of Job's life *not* governed by his desire to love the Lord and to follow his will. Job was "upright" in his actions, honest and faithful in all he did. He "feared God and turned away from evil." To fear God means to love, respect, and obey him. The person who fears God turns away from what God says is wrong, which is what Job did. (1:1)

This description of Job was not the writer's personal opinion or the general opinion of Job's friends. Rather, it was God's description of Job. God twice described Job this way (Job 1:8; 2:3). And since the book was written after God spoke these words, at the beginning of chap-

5

ter 1, the writer was using God's own words to describe Job.

We are told that Job was a very rich man. He had a large family, a great number of flocks and herds, and many servants. Job was "the greatest of all the men of the East" (Job 1:3). He was unsurpassed in possessions and authority among the people of the land.

In these opening verses, we are told about the depth of Job's faith. He had grown children, and his children met regularly to celebrate important occasions. Job understood what could happen when people are eating and drinking and enjoying themselves. He said, "Perhaps my children have sinned and cursed God in their hearts" (Job 1:5). Therefore, after their celebrations, Job would offer a sacrifice for each of his children and ask God to forgive them if they had sinned. Job did this regularly; his concern for his children's salvation never let up.

This shows that Job understood sin and forgiveness—his children's sins and his own sins. The act of making a sacrifice for forgiveness demonstrated that Job understood the basics of the true religion of the true God: People cannot make up for their own sin; they need the sacrifice of another. Job understood God's forgiving love and was confident that God would accept his sacrifices. (1:2-5)

God's challenge to Satan

Job's life of faith in God's loving forgiveness and the many blessings he had received from God form the starting point for the claim Satan would soon make.

One day in heaven "the sons of God came to present themselves before the LORD, and Satan also came into their midst" (Job 1:6). Literally, the verse refers to Satan as "the satan," which can be translated "the accuser." God and Satan had a conversation about Job. Their conversation illustrated something Satan does, namely, that he accuses God's people of having a false faith and being worthy of God's just judgment.

Significantly, it was not Satan who started the conversation, however. Satan said he had been walking around on earth, but he didn't say why. He didn't mention Job as a person he was planning to attack. He didn't say something like, "I just saw Job, the greatest hypocrite on earth. He doesn't love you; he loves the things you have given to him. Let me prove it to you."

Rather, the text says it was God who started the ball rolling. After Satan told God that he had been roaming throughout the earth, God brought Job to Satan's attention: "Have you considered my servant Job? There is no one like him on the earth, a man who is blameless and upright, who fears God and turns away from evil" (Job 1:8). It would be like a young man walking into a basketball scrimmage and yelling out, "I'm the best shooter in the world." He didn't make a direct challenge to the others, but they would all take it that way. They would challenge him to prove it.

God boasted about Job: "See what my grace has done. See how important my mercy and forgiveness are to Job." Job was a model believer about whom God could say, "There is no one like him on the earth" (Job 1:8). We should keep God's appraisal of Job in mind when

7

later we hear Job's friends and Elihu lecture Job about such things as morality and chastisement.

God's challenge to Satan was implicit, but it was a challenge, no less. Satan promptly took the bait. He accused Job of a "health and wealth" faith: "Is it without cause that Job fears God?" (Job 1:9). Job loves you, Satan was saying, not because of what he sees in you but because you've given him so many earthly blessings.

Satan then offered a direct challenge: "Stretch out your hand and strike everything that is his, and he will certainly curse you to your face!" (Job 1:11). "Very well, then," God responded. "Everything that he has is in your hand. But you may not stretch out your hand against the man himself" (Job 1:12). Therefore, we see that Satan challenged God, but it was only after God had held up Job as a sincere, God-fearing man.

Once he got the green light, Satan lost no time. The events that followed took place in a single day. All Job's oxen and donkeys were taken away. His flocks perished along with the servants who watched them. All his camels were stolen, and the servants who cared for them died by the sword. Worst of all, all Job's children died when a windstorm collapsed the house where they were feasting—and without their father having had the chance to sacrifice for them.

Job was struck with sorrow. He expressed deep grief by tearing his clothes and shaving his head, as the ancients did. But nonetheless, he glorified God. He fell on the ground and worshiped God: "Naked I came from my mother's womb, and naked I will return. The LORD gave

and the LORD has taken away. May the name of the
LORD be blessed" (Job 1:21).

The writer closes with these significant words: "In all
this, Job did not sin or blame God" (Job 1:22). Later,
God would rebuke Job for the sin of wrongly accusing
him of injustice. But at this point, despite losing everything he owned and his ten children, Job did not commit that sin. He did not "attribute any impropriety to
God" (Job 1:22).[1] Just the opposite. Job glorified God as
he had done before. (1:6-22)

Special Topic: Old Testament Faith

How did Job and others in the ancient non-Israelite
world learn about God's promise of a Savior?

Had the message been written down? Possibly, but we
have no record of that. Was it common knowledge?
There is no doubt that the promise was passed down by
word of mouth. If Job had lived at the time of Abraham
or the patriarchs, he might have been aware of them and
even heard about the special promises they had received
from God. But that remains speculation.

For these reasons, we might think that the ancients'
knowledge of God and his salvation was incomplete
and ill-defined. Yet that is far from the truth. Job himself is a good example of that. James encouraged New
Testament believers to take to heart Job's example of
perseverance in faith: "As you know, we consider blessed

---

[1] This is an alternate translation. See the EHV footnote for this
verse.

those who have persevered. You have heard of Job's perseverance and have seen what the Lord finally brought about. The Lord is full of compassion and mercy" (James 5:11 NIV84). James would not have urged New Testament Christians to take the example of a person whose faith was incomplete and ill-defined.

And consider Melchizedek, a great man who was a contemporary of Abraham. He was an ancient priest in Jerusalem, long before God created the Old Testament priesthood through Moses. His position likely included teaching residents of the city about God's promises. In chapters 5, 6, and 7 of Hebrews, the writer explains the similarity between Melchizedek and Christ: Melchizedek "is first, by translation of his name, king of righteousness, and then he is also king of Salem, that is, king of peace" (Hebrews 7:2). We are not told how well Melchizedek understood the connection between his name and the work of the coming Savior. But considering the praise he received from Abraham and the writer of Hebrews, he might have understood that his name pictured the coming Savior, who is our righteousness and our peace. Considering the fact that he accepted Abraham's tithes, he likely understood his exalted place in God's plan of salvation, which surpassed even that of Abraham and Abraham's descendants. He may have known that he was the head of a priesthood in which Christ would serve—greater than the priesthood of Aaron and his sons who served the people of Israel under Moses' Law.

Jesus and the New Testament writers used Old Testament people of faith to encourage New Testament Christians, like James used Job. Abraham is the best example. God had promised to bless Abraham. Abraham lacked details about how God would fulfill his promise. Nevertheless, Jesus told the Jewish people, "Your father Abraham rejoiced that he would see my day. He saw it and was glad" (John 8:56). There is no clearer way of saying that even though Abraham lacked the historical details, his faith was faith in Christ, and that it was full and complete.

Similarly, Paul helps us understand our own faith by describing the nature of Abraham's faith,

> What then shall we say was gained by Abraham, our forefather according to the flesh? For if Abraham was justified by works, he has something to boast about, but not before God. For what does the Scripture say? "Abraham believed God, and it was counted to him as righteousness." (Romans 4:1-3)

Paul also spoke about the depth of Abraham's faith. He said that Abraham was aware of a truth that at first was unclear to many New Testament believers, namely, that the Gospel was also meant for all people. In fact, the early Christian Church in Jerusalem had to hold councils to make it clear that Jews were saved by faith alone and that Gentile believers were also members of the Church and were also saved by faith alone (Acts 11 and 15). Paul wrote:

> Know then that it is those of faith who are the sons of Abraham. And the Scripture, *foreseeing that God would justify the Gentiles by faith*, preached the gospel beforehand to Abraham, saying, *"In you shall all the nations be blessed."* So then, those who are of faith are blessed along with Abraham, the man of faith. (Galatians 3:7-9)

11

The writer of Hebrews equated Old Testament faith and New Testament faith. He spoke about Moses' faith before God told him to deliver the Israelites from Egypt. The writer said that Moses' faith was faith in Christ:

> By faith Moses, when he was grown up, refused to be called the son of Pharaoh's daughter, choosing rather to be mistreated with the people of God than to enjoy the fleeting pleasures of sin. He considered the reproach *of Christ* greater wealth than the treasures of Egypt, for he was looking to the reward. (Hebrews 11:24-26)

Abraham knew he would someday be in heaven, like Job did. The writer of Hebrews tells us about his faith in God's promise of everlasting life:

> By faith [Abraham] went to live in the land of promise, as in a foreign land, living in tents with Isaac and Jacob, heirs with him of the same promise. For he was looking forward to the city that has foundations, whose designer and builder is God. (Hebrews 11:9,10)

The writer of Hebrews also used the faith of many Old Testament believers to encourage us. He said that Abel offered a better sacrifice than Cain, doing so "by faith" (Hebrews 11:4). He continued by pointing out that Enoch pleased God by faith in his promises. Noah built an ark because he believed God when God told him about a coming flood. Rahab was not killed along with the other residents of Jericho when it fell before the Israelites because she had faith in the God of Israel.

The saints in the Old Testament looked forward to the Savior's arrival, by whom we and they are *made perfect*:

All these people were still living by faith when they died. They did not receive the things promised; they only saw them and welcomed them from a distance. And they admitted that they were aliens and strangers on earth. People who say such things show that they are looking for a country of their own. If they had been thinking of the country they had left, they would have had opportunity to return. Instead, they were longing for a better country—a heavenly one. Therefore God is not ashamed to be called their God, for he has prepared a city for them. (Hebrews 11:13-16 NIV84)

These were all commended for their faith, yet none of them received what had been promised. God had planned something better for us so that only together with us would they be made perfect. (Hebrews 11:39,40 NIV84)

When we think about the faith of Old Testament believers, we should not think in terms of ancient cultures and how detailed was their historical knowledge of God's plan of salvation. We should think in terms of having faith in the promised Savior and serving God according to his will. This was the faith Job had and it was the basis of his life. This will become clearer when we watch Job persevere in faith in the face of his suffering.

Job Glorified God Again—Job 2

Getting Into the Book

Reading—Chapter 2

Job 2 Job's second trial

Verses 1-6

> We are introduced to another scene in heaven like the scene we saw in chapter 1. Satan came before God. God pointed out that Job continued to maintain his integrity despite his sufferings. His faith and service to God remained firm. God's statement about Job elicited another counter challenge from Satan. If God struck Job's body, Satan said, Job would reject him. God allowed Satan to carry out the terms of his challenge. But the suffering could not be severe enough to kill him.

Verses 7-10

> Satan struck Job with a horrible disease. Even Job's wife tried to influence Job to curse God. Job contin-

ued to praise God and did not blame him for being unfair.

Verses 11–13

Three of Job's friends came to comfort him. They were dumbfounded at the degree of Job's suffering, and for seven days they sat in silence.

Looking at Job

Job's sufferings increase

Once again the angels presented themselves before God in heaven. Once again Satan was present. And once again God started a conversation with him about Job.

For the third time Job was described as "a man who is blameless and upright, who fears God and turns away from evil" (Job 2:3). So far, God had won. Job not only refused to give up his faith. He praised God in his time of loss just as he had in his time of plenty. God prefaced his praise of Job by saying, "There is no one like him on the earth" (Job 2:3). In wisdom and firmness of faith, Job surpassed all his contemporaries. Not only was Job blameless, but he also maintained his blamelessness even after God "destroyed him for no reason" (Job 2:3). There was a reason, of course, why God afflicted Job. He wanted to prove to Satan the sincerity of Job's faith. What God meant in this verse was that Job had committed no sin that led God to make him suffer. We should keep that phrase in mind since it is directly related to God's justice. We will come back to this verse throughout this book.

Job had lost all his possessions, and his children were gone, but as God said, "He still maintains his integrity, even though you incited me against him to destroy him for no reason" (Job 2:3). The word "integrity" encompasses everything we have heard three times now about Job's character. He continued to love and respect God and to serve him sincerely with all his heart. He refused to curse God for all the suffering God had brought into his life.

God's praise of Job could not go unanswered. As before, Satan took this as a challenge. Let's up the stakes, Satan suggested: "Skin for skin! A man will give all he has for his life. But stretch out your hand and strike his bones and flesh, and he will certainly curse you to your face!" (Job 2:4,5). God went along with Satan's challenge and allowed Satan to afflict Job with bodily pain—up to the point of death, but no further. So Satan "struck Job with very painful sores from the sole of his foot to the top of his head," and "Job took a piece of broken pottery to scrape himself as he was sitting among the ashes" (Job 2:7,8).

Job glorifies God a second time

Job's wife had had enough. When they lost their possessions and family, she seems to have followed Job's lead patiently. But when she saw her husband suffering as he was, she gave in to the sin Satan wanted Job to commit: "Are you still maintaining your integrity? Curse God and die!" (Job 2:9). But even at the urging of his wife, Job would not budge. He replied, "You are talking like a woman who lacks moral judgment. If we accept the good that comes from God, shouldn't we also accept the

17

bad?" (Job 2:10). Once again, the writer records the victory of God's grace over Satan's claims: "In all this, Job did not sin in what he said" (Job 2:10). Job did not do as Satan said he would, namely, curse God to his face. Nor did he fall into the sin he would later commit, namely, saying that God was dealing with him unjustly.

Job's friends arrive

After Job had shown complete acceptance of the suffering God brought on him, three of his friends arrived. We don't know how long it was between when Job started to suffer and when his friends arrived to comfort him. Their purpose was to "sympathize with Job and to comfort him" (Job 2:11). When they saw Job, they could only weep. "Each man tore his robe and tossed dust into the air and onto his head. They sat on the ground with him for seven days and seven nights, but no one spoke a word to him because they saw that his suffering was very great" (Job 2:12,13). Some say that the friends were showing Job respect by remaining silent. But the text says that they were silent because of what they saw before them. They were dumbfounded at how greatly Job was suffering, and they had nothing to say.

Job was forced to break the silence. Immediately Job began to complain about what God was doing to him. Sometimes we focus on Job's complaints too quickly. We say, "Yes, Job was a patient man. But he was troubled with doubts, complained bitterly, and questioned God's justice." But as we have seen, Job started to complain only after he had shown perfect resignation to God's plans for a long time.

A final point about Job's struggle with his friends: As we will see, Job's three friends put Job through a painful spiritual struggle. Some say that Satan was behind this additional trial, just as he had been behind Job's first two trials. But we are not told that it was Satan who sent the three friends. God had given him permission to take away Job's wealth and then send him terrible bodily suffering. But that's all. After chapter 2, Satan is not mentioned. We dare not give him a greater place in the book of Job than the writer gives him. While Job's losses and bodily suffering were miraculous, the suffering Job's friends caused him didn't need a miracle. It came in a very human way. The friends caused him to suffer by tempting him to think about God in a false way. And as we will see, it is a very normal thing for human beings, including Job, to find this error to be enticing—even without Satan's help.

~~~

Special Topic: Who Sends Suffering?

Sometimes people do wicked things that naturally result in suffering. For example, they abuse their bodies and suffer the results. They may break the law and suffer a penalty. They may act in a loveless way and suffer rejection. But often their suffering comes to them like it came to Job. Through no fault of their own, they suffer loss of property or a loved one, or they are in an accident that leaves them debilitated. When that kind of suffering comes into their lives, they ask where it came from. They want to know who sent it.

There are two ways we can answer that question. Either God sent it, or Satan sent it. Since suffering is bad, we naturally don't want to think that our good and merciful God sent it. It's easier to think that it came from Satan.

Sometimes we attempt to keep God in the picture by saying that God *allowed* Satan to send the suffering and add that God showed his power by setting a limit on what Satan was allowed to do.

Before we settle for that answer, though, let's ask that question of the people in the book of Job, including Satan and God himself. Who caused the events that made Job suffer?

According to Job. After he experienced the loss of everything he owned, Job said; "Naked I came from my mother's womb, and naked I will return. The Lᴏʀᴅ gave and the Lᴏʀᴅ has taken away. May the name of the Lᴏʀᴅ be blessed" (Job 1:21). After his bodily disease began, he said, "If we accept the good *that comes from God*, shouldn't we also accept the bad?" (Job 2:10). Throughout the book, Job continued to say that God brought suffering into his life. In fact, every time we as Christians quote Job—"The Lᴏʀᴅ gave and the Lord has taken away"—we too are confessing that God is behind the loss or suffering we are enduring.

According to God. When God spoke with Satan the second time, he said,

> Have you considered my servant Job? There is no one like him on the earth, a man who is blameless and upright, who fears God and turns away from evil. And he still maintains his integrity, even though you incited *me* against him to destroy him for no reason." (Job 2:3)

Satan had a role in Job's suffering, but God said that he was the one who was making Job suffer.

According to Satan. When Satan challenged God the first time, he said that if Job lost everything, he would curse God. Here's how he made the challenge: "But just stretch out *your* hand and strike everything that is his, and he will certainly curse *you* to your face!" (Job 1:11). When Satan issued his second challenge, he addressed God in a similar way: "Skin for skin! A man will give all he has for his life. But stretch out *your* hand and strike his bones and flesh, and he will certainly curse *you* to your face!" (Job 2:4,5).

Both times Satan confessed that God had afflicted Job and could do so again. It's not accurate to say, "Satan has plans for us, but God allows him to go only so far." We should rather say, "God has plans for us. which he carries out. And if he wishes, he uses Satan and his evil desires as his tool to carry out his plans." Only in that sense does he "allow" Satan to bring evil into a person's life.

It is difficult to keep God and Satan neatly separated when it comes to what happens in a person's life. We might say, "What happened to me was God's plan, not Satan's." Yet Scripture says that Satan too has plans for us. Or we might say, "The plan is God's, but the evil involved in that plan came from Satan." Even though that does not answer all the problems involved with God and suffering, that way of speaking seems to better reflect what happened in Job 1 and 2.

According to Job's wife. Job's wife attributed Job's suffering to God: "Then his wife said to him, 'Are you still maintaining your integrity? Curse *God* and die!'" (Job 2:9).

According to Job's friends. Job's friends said that God sent suffering into Job's life because that's what Job deserved. Eliphaz said; "This is what I have observed: Those who plow evil and sow trouble will reap the same. By the breath of God they perish. By the blast from his nostrils they come to an end" (Job 4:8,9). Also, there was no doubt in Elihu's mind that Job's suffering came from God. The friends were wrong about why God sent suffering into Job's life. But they were right in saying that God sent it. Again, note that Satan is not mentioned after Job's friends arrived.

According to Job's family and acquaintances. After God restored Job, we hear what his relatives and acquaintances thought about the source of Job's suffering: "Then all his brothers and sisters and all his acquaintances visited Job. They dined with him in his house, and they showed him sympathy and comforted him concerning *the tragedy that the LORD had brought on him*" (Job 42:11).

To some, the idea that God is behind our suffering is jolting. No one wants to blame God for a tragic event and the suffering that comes with it. But that is far more comforting than the idea that Satan has plans for us and that God passively sits back and sets limits to what Satan can do. Again, the relationship between God's plans and Satan's plans is sometimes hard to understand, but we must be careful not to lead a suffering person to think that Satan has the final authority over anything that happens in their life.

In Lamentations, Jeremiah confessed the same thing that Job confessed: "Who has spoken and it came to pass, unless the Lord has commanded it? Is it not from the mouth of the Most High that good and bad come?" (Lamentations 3:37,38). Only when we recognize this fact can we counsel the suffering person to direct their prayers to God and ask for his help. August Pieper said that this fact is "the basis upon which alone any spiritual treatment can succeed." He wrote, "*God has sent this!* In the book of Job this is the self-evident presupposition of all the persons involved" and, "In all cases, it should be the basis—both for the pastor and for the patient—of any conversation between them."[2]

---

[2] August Pieper, "The Book of Job in Its Significance for Preaching and the Care of Souls," trans. James Fricke and Armin Schuetze, (*Wisconsin Lutheran Quarterly*, Vol. 57 (1960), pp. 50-71, 118-141, 197-219. This citation is from the updated version by Rev. Tom Jeske, Seminary Essay Files, p. 39.

Chapter 3

God Vindicated Job—Job 42

Getting Into the Book

Reading—Chapter 42

Job 42 *God's Vindication of Job*

Verses 1-6

After God was finished rebuking Job, Job confessed his sin of questioning God's ways. He confessed:

You can do all things and nothing you do can be questioned.

You challenged me to defend what I ignorantly said about you. I criticized your plans, but I didn't know what I was talking about. I was forming conclusions about things way over my head.

I wanted to question you about my suffering, but I couldn't find you. Now you have come to me, and you are the one asking the questions. All I can do is despise myself and repent for the ignorant way I spoke about you.

Verses 7–9

> God vindicated Job's faith and said that his friends' teaching about him was wrong. Job served as God's agent to offer sacrifices on their behalf and to pray for them. God accepted Job's sacrifices and his prayers.

Verses 10–17

> Job's family and acquaintances visited him and gave him gifts. God blessed Job with twice as much as he had before. Job's three daughters were singled out as great blessings. Job saw his children and grand-children to the fourth generation. And he died after living a long and fulfilled life.

Looking at Job

Scripture vindicates Job

At this point, we jump to the end of the book, where the poetry ends and the prose begins again. Note that Job 42:1-6 is written in poetry and technically is in the central part of the book. But in these verses and in the rest of chapter 42, we find information that will help us understand the conversation and the book as a whole, so we'll cover it here.

In chapter 42, Job's life of service to God and his understanding of God are vindicated. Job had not fallen into the errors of his friends. He had persevered in his faith and had never given up his integrity. He had sinned by calling God unjust, but he quickly repented when God pointed out his error.

Before we look more closely at chapter 42, let's look at how James and Ezekiel spoke about Job and in the process vindicated him.

James 5:11. James uses Job to inspire all God's people to persevere in faith. James remembered Job, not for his sin of questioning God's ways but for his perseverance in the faith.

To understand James' encouragement to us, it is important to look at a particular phrase James uses. The New International Version (NIV) translates James 5:11 like this: "As you know, we count as blessed those who have persevered. You have heard of Job's perseverance and have seen what the Lord finally brought about. The Lord is full of compassion and mercy."

The words the NIV translates, "what the Lord finally brought about," is a paraphrase of the Greek, which simply says, "the end of the Lord." The "end of the Lord" can be understood in two ways. It can be understood as referring to the *purpose* for which God sent suffering into Job's life (which, as some claim, might include his desire to chasten Job or strengthen his faith in some way). The English Standard Version (ESV) agrees with this paraphrase and translates like this: "And you have seen the *purpose* of the Lord."

On the other hand, it can be understood as the *final result* of what happened to Job, referring to how God vindicated Job and richly blessed him after his sufferings were over, as described in Job 42. The NIV, quoted above, translates the word in that sense: "what the Lord *finally brought about.*"

27

The NIV translation seems more natural in the context. In the next sentence James wrote, "The Lord is full of compassion and mercy" (James 5:11). James is saying that God richly blessed Job, and if we persevere like Job did, our "end" will be the same as his. That is, God will bless us like he blessed Job.

This also fits well with what James wrote in the previous verse: "As an example of suffering and patience, brothers, take the prophets who spoke in the name of the Lord" (James 5:10). The prophets' sufferings were not sent to chasten them but came on them because they proclaimed God's Word. Job suffered for the same reason. He persevered in believing God's promises.

Ezekiel 14. The second place in which Job is mentioned outside the book of Job is Ezekiel 14. Ezekiel referred to Job several times but mentions him by name in two sections:

> Son of man [God addressing Ezekiel], when a land sins against me by acting faithlessly, and I stretch out my hand against it and break its supply of bread and send famine upon it, and cut off from it man and beast, even if these three men, Noah, Daniel, and Job, were in it, they would deliver but their own lives by their righteousness, declares the Lord GOD. (verses 13,14)

> Or if I send a pestilence into that land and pour out my wrath upon it with blood, to cut off from it man and beast, even if Noah, Daniel, and Job were in it, as I live, declares the Lord GOD, they would deliver neither son nor daughter. They would deliver but their own lives by their righteousness. (verses 19,20)

God puts Job in a group with Noah and Daniel. All three lived upright lives and exercised great patience. "Noah was a righteous man, blameless in his generation" (Genesis 6:9). For the many years he built the ark, Noah perseveringly bore witness to God's impending judgment on the world.

Daniel was a man "greatly loved" by God (Daniel 9:23) and he faithfully served God throughout Israel's 70-year captivity in Babylon. He persevered, waiting for God to deliver Israel from Babylon as he had promised. And for years he lived with the possibility that a new king might kill him for worshiping the true God.

Job fits well in this group. He was a righteous man who patiently held on to his faith amid severe suffering.

The Lord, through Ezekiel and James, linked Job to others who were examples of righteous believers. Job's sins and the sins of Noah and Daniel—and they did sin—were not in view. They were new creations of God, men who refused to give up their faith when God, whose love they knew, made them go through times of great difficulty. Even if these three men were alive in his day, Ezekiel explained to his readers, they would not benefit the people of Israel. The land would be saved only if the current generation trusted in God and served him as these three men did. In the process of saying this, God put his stamp of approval on the faith of these three men.

God vindicates Job before his three friends

In the present chapter, Job 42, God made it clear to all that he approved of Job's faith and life, and that it was an example they should all follow.

God rebuked Job for complaining about his wisdom, but in the process of the rebuke, God showed himself to Job in a new way. Job had heard about God in his Word just like we do. But in chapters 38–42:6, we learn that God spoke to Job directly "out of a violent storm" (Job 38:1). We cannot be sure if God appeared to Job in some special form, yet God appeared to him in such a way that Job could say, "My ear heard about you. Now my eyes see you" (Job 42:5). This demonstrated to Job that God had not abandoned him because of his sinful complaining. He was still God's child. He still had God's forgiveness and the hope of eternal life. Job learned that he *could* repent of his sins and be sure of God's forgiveness. And that is what Job did: "So I despise myself. I repent in dust and ashes" (Job 42:6).

God vindicated Job in the face of his friends' accusations. They had claimed that Job was suffering because of a sin he was secretly committing. Elihu claimed that God was chastening Job for that sin. But after God rebuked him, did Job repent of some sin like they had in mind? Job did repent of a sin, but it was not some sin that led God to afflict him. Rather, he repented of a sin he committed *after* he was well along in his suffering—the sin of claiming that God was unjust to make him suffer. Job said: "I know that you can do all things. No purpose of yours can be thwarted. . . . I have made statements about things I did not understand, things too wonderful for me to know" (Job 42:2,3). If Job had been suffering because of some special sin, as his friends claimed, it would be reasonable to say that God would have brought up Job's need to repent of that sin as well. But God was silent about anything other than Job's claim that God was unjust. Job was, in fact, the blameless and upright man God said he was in chapters 1 and 2.

The first thing God did after he rebuked Job was address Job's friends. He turned to Eliphaz and rebuked him: "My anger burns against you and your two friends, because none of you have spoken correctly about me, as my servant Job did" (Job 42:7).

The friends did not understand the way God works. They thought they were speaking wisely, but they were not. Their error was *not* that they falsely accused Job, although they did that too. Rather, it was that they did not speak correctly about *God*. God's mercy and forgiveness played little or no role in their advice to Job. Except for Eliphaz' brief statement that it was a blessing to be corrected by God (Job 5:17), they all told Job that he was getting what he deserved, and that God would bless him only if he regained God's favor by giving up his sin. They taught what we call "work-righteousness," which wrongly said that Job could earn back God's favor, and that God would no longer be compelled to punish him.

On the other hand, despite his sin of questioning God's wisdom, Job understood God and spoke about him correctly. He knew God's forgiving love, and that's what prompted his service to God. He did not live an innocent life to gain wealth; he did so because he loved God.

31

Accordingly, he refused to give up his integrity—his ongoing desire to love God and shun evil—even when his riches were gone. Nor would he deny his integrity, as if it didn't exist. If he did that, he would have denied the love of God that had elicited his righteous life. In that respect, Job never spoke wrongly about God. Job persevered in his faith and fought off all temptations to abandon God even though God was afflicting an innocent man with terrible suffering.

Job 42 continues with God's solution to the sin Job's three friends had committed. God told Eliphaz:

> So now, take seven bulls and seven rams for yourselves, go to my servant Job, and offer up a whole burnt offering for yourselves. My servant Job will pray for you, so that I will look upon him with favor and not deal with you on the basis of your foolishness, for none of you have spoken correctly about me, as my servant Job did." (verse 8)

This reflects the sacrificial system God gave his people, Israel. Job likely lived before God gave this system to Israel, but the principle of offering a sacrifice for sin was present in the world since the days of Adam and Eve. Job was to act as God's priest. The friends were to bring animals for a "whole burnt offering." In the Old Testament sacrificial system, the whole burnt offering was the only offering that was completely burned up—totally given to the Lord. It was to demonstrate complete devotion to the Lord. Job had offered complete devotion to the Lord. But the friends had only a partial, worldly understanding of God and true service to him. Their whole burnt offering expressed their desire to give themselves completely to God, like Job had.

The friends were to bring their offering to Job. Job would pray for them. God would look favorably on the actions of his true servant, Job, and he would forgive the sins of the friends. God would not give them what they deserved, which, ironically, the friends thought he was doing to Job.

Then God explained the nature of their sin a second time: "I will . . . not deal with you on the basis of *your foolishness,* for *none of you have spoken correctly about me,* as my servant Job did" (Job 42:8).

The writer of Job continues, "So Eliphaz the Temanite, Bildad the Shuhite, and Zophar the Na'amathite went and did as the LORD had told them, and the LORD looked on Job with favor" (Job 42:9). Notice the striking way the writer put that. He might have said, "So the Lord looked with favor on the three friends because they obeyed God and brought a sacrifice as God commanded." But the obedience of the three friends was not the reason for God's favor. Rather, Job was serving as their priest, and the Lord accepted the three friends because he looked with favor on Job.

This reflects the nature of the gospel. Most important is not our sacrifice to God—our actions, our words, our deeds of love. What is most important is the priest God has given us, namely Jesus, and the sacrifice he made for us. God looks with favor on his Son and blesses us for Jesus' sake, as we pray.

The friends now saw Job for who he was. Four times in two verses (Job 42:7,8), God called Job "my servant" as he had done twice in his earlier conversations with Satan. Job had been God's servant when Satan made

33

his challenge. He remained God's servant throughout the long discussion with his friends when, despite his sin of accusing God of injustice, he spoke correctly about God's mercy. He remained God's servant after his suffering when he acted as God's priest on behalf of his three friends.

Sometimes we treat Job's three friends as rank unbelievers. But were they? They were very work-righteous, which was why they couldn't speak rightly about God. But consider the following. First, they were Job's friends. It would be hard to imagine Job having close friends who outright rejected God, whom Job loved so much. Second, much of what they said was true. In the New Testament Paul even quoted what Eliphaz said regarding God's judgment (1 Corinthians 3:19, see Job 5:13). While Eliphaz wrongly applied this to Job, the statement was true, and, as Paul said, it spoke correctly about God's final judgment on unbelievers. Third, God told the three friends to bring sacrifices and promised that he would "not deal with [them] on the basis of [their] foolishness" (Job 42:8). Therefore, the three friends must have known about such things as sin, repentance, sacrifice for sin, and God's forgiveness.

God did not cast off these men, though he could have. He was concerned about them and gave them the peace they withheld from Job. Now they felt the joy of God's forgiveness of their own sins. And perhaps they realized from this how they could have done a better job of comforting Job.

God vindicates Job before the world

After God vindicated Job to his three friends, he vindicated Job to the world. Job had said earlier that many thought of him like the friends did—that God was punishing him for some great and secret sin—and they despised him. (See Job 28:1-10.)

His family and acquaintances met at his home to give him the sympathy and comfort that his three friends withheld. They gave him some money and a ring to show him their respect and affection. They no longer inferred from his suffering that he was being punished or chastened by God.

God also vindicated Job's faith and life by giving him twice as much as he had given Job before. God replaced the children he had taken out of his life. Note that God did not give Job twice as many children. To do so would have undermined the fact that his first children had risen and were now enjoying life with God.

The writer focused on the beauty of Job's daughters. They were noble women, worthy of an inheritance along with their brothers. It is hard to say why the writer called attention to their beauty. Perhaps it was because when people looked at them, they were reminded of the beauty of their father's faith and perseverance.

Job was "fulfilled by a long life" (Job 42:17). God blessed Job by giving him a long life filled with the joy of many offspring. God had taken much away from Job and had brought him to the doorstep of death. But the blessings God gave Job and the many years God gave Job to enjoy them assured Job that God had not forsaken him.

35

~~~

Special Topic: Job's Perseverance; Christian Perseverance

Job persevered throughout his time of suffering. But what does it mean to persevere in suffering?

Perseverance is not just sticking it out, trying to not complain, or keeping a positive outlook. Rather, it means enduring suffering without the suffering causing one to lose confidence in God or deny him. It is never to allow suffering to make one give up their hope in Christ's forgiveness. It is to suffer but at the same time to strive to serve God with heart, soul, and mind.

But we all know the challenges that face everyone who is called to do that. The book of Job helps us understand those challenges. Job's natural temptations to complain and question God; the reaction of his wife; the scorn of his household servants and acquaintances; the teaching of his friends, which made it impossible for him to find peace with God—all contributed to his struggle. And in some way, these are elements in the challenge that all suffering people face.

The Scripture writer, James, urges us to find encouragement from the account of Job and to imitate his perseverance. Let's think about the depth of Job's perseverance.

This is important because Job's complaints against God and his charges of injustice are part of the long discussion between Job and his friends. These complaints can skew our view of Job and argue against his perseverance.

Suffering came into Job's life in the first two chapters. Throughout those chapters, his perseverance was perfect. He continued to confess God's right to give and take away, to send bad as well as good things into a person's life. He continued to praise God in suffering as he had praised him in good times.

But at the end of chapter 2, Job's friends arrived to comfort him. Then follow 35 chapters of conversation—debate, actually—between Job and his friends. From that point on, even though Job continued to persevere, he began to question the justice of how God was dealing with him, which is the sin for which God rebuked him in the final chapters of the book.

Unless you think about it, it seems as if the first part of Job's suffering was relatively short and the second period was long—2 chapters versus 35 chapters. How wonderfully Job persevered in faith throughout the first period! But those chapters are over quickly, and the rest of Job's speeches are marred by complaints and charges of injustice against God. Because of this, it is easy to downplay or skip over Job's perseverance in the first period of his suffering and become focused on the sin of questioning God that he committed in the second period.

But where should our focus lie? On Job's praise or on Job's complaints? It helps to think about the relative length of time it took for those two periods to take place.

Consider the first period covered by Job 1 and 2. Satan lost no time in making Job suffer, and the losses all happened on the same day. As soon as one servant had reported a catastrophe, another servant arrived to report another, the last being the loss of his children. These were not partial losses. Everything was gone.

This was the test Satan suggested. But in order for it to be a test, a sufficient amount of time had to pass before it became clear whether or not Job would react to his losses in a God-pleasing way. Of course, only God knew how long the test had to last. But a week or two of living with the loss of all his things would not be long enough to test Job's love for God—at least one would think that. The same could be said about this second test. Time had to pass before it could be shown that God was right about Job and that Satan was wrong.

Accordingly, the events of chapters 1 and 2 must have taken place over a relatively long period of time. Again, we don't know how long, but Job gives us a hint. Near the beginning of the conversation, Job said to his friends:

> Isn't man's time on earth like being compelled to serve in the army?
> Aren't his days like those of a hired man?
> Like a slave, he longs for shade,
> or like a day laborer, he waits for his pay.
> In the same way, *I have been allotted months of futility*,
> and nights of agony have been assigned to me.
> (Job 7:1-3)

What is more, it would have taken a fair amount of time for the friends to learn about Job's suffering, agree with each other to visit him, prepare for the trip, and make the journey. That likely would not have been a matter of days or weeks, but of months.

Compare this with how long the 35 chapters of conversation might have lasted. A conversation naturally flows from one person to the next and from one topic to the next. The conversation in Job is a long one, so it may have taken several days or as much as a few weeks. There are pauses noted in the conversation. However, it seems odd to envision those pauses extending over a long time. Nor does it seem natural for each of the men to spend days organizing their thoughts before they presented their next speech. Moreover, Job's friends didn't have to carefully organize their thoughts every time they talked because they said essentially the same thing in all of their speeches.

The conversation is written in poetry, which would have taken a longer time to compose. Some say that the conversation was spoken in normal prose but that the writer of the book turned it into poetry. If this is true, the idea that it took at least several days for the speakers to put their thoughts into poetic language does not hold.

Therefore, the first part of the book, short as it is, spanned a much longer time than long second part. Job lived months with loss and bodily suffering before the conversation began. Throughout that whole time, he continued to glorify God and did not accuse God of injustice. When we later hear Job start to question God, we should always remember the previous longer time period during which he confessed: "The LORD gave and the LORD has taken away. May the name of the LORD be blessed" (Job 1:21) and, "If we accept the good that comes from God, shouldn't we also accept the bad?" (Job 2:10). During this period, we witness perfect perseverance—the kind of perseverance James urged us to imitate. During this time Job "did not sin or blame God" and he "did not sin in what he said" (Job 1:22; 2:10). It would have only been in the relatively short time when he was conversing with his friends that he started to struggle and demand that God give him the reason for his suffering.

There is another aspect of Job's perseverance that we learn about in the conversation. For Job, the suffering itself was terribly hard. Harder still, however, was facing friends who misunderstood God, put no emphasis on God's forgiveness, and claimed that all suffering is a direct result of a sin the sufferer is committing.

Job's hardest challenge was to know that God still loved him and forgave him and to maintain the fact that he had served God faithfully—all the while being told that God *always* sends suffering to correct sin. Under the influence of his friends Job found himself caught between two ways of understanding God. He was in a vise with two jaws, the jaw of a merciful and blessing-filled God and the jaw of a God who seemed distant, uncaring, and unjust.

Job knew his friends were wrong. But his friends' logic was persuasive, and Job was tempted to use their logic in analyzing why God was making him suffer. In one of his speeches Job said:

> I cry out, "Injustice," but I get no answer.
> I call for help, but there is no justice.
> He has blocked my way, so I cannot get by.
> He has brought darkness on my paths.
> He has stripped me of my honor,
> and he has taken the crown off my head.

He tears me down on every side, until I am gone.
He uproots my hope like a tree.
His anger burns against me,
and he regards me as his enemy. (Job 19:7-11)

It seemed to Job that God's love had been replaced by God's anger, which was burning against him. It seemed that his former friend had become his enemy.

That's how it seemed to Job. From the first two chapters of the book, however, we know that God was actually cheering Job on: "Persevere in your faith in my goodness. Although your suffering seems to prove the opposite, I am here. My love for you continues unabated."

But Job didn't know that. At first Job persevered by holding on to the true God he had known his whole life. But under the influence of his friends, Job found himself caught between confidence and doubt. There now seemed to be two Gods, the God of mercy and the God of pure justice. God seemed to be in opposition to God. Job's call was to persevere in his original understanding of how God deals with people and reject how his friends were explaining God's actions.

This struggle is the heart of the book of Job. If Job had let the thoughts of his friends determine his relationship with God, Satan would have won. But if Job drove those thoughts out of his mind and persevered in his faith in God's love and mercy—if he held on to his integrity and remained God's servant—then God won.

Job does not describe his faith in the Savior in the first two chapters of the book. But when forced to counter his friends' false teaching and maintain his love for God, he knew there was only one way: by holding on to his knowledge of God's promise of a Savior. Job's complaints seem to dominate. But, in fact, it's Job's expressions of faith that dominate. This is where we hear the real Job speaking, and this is also where we find our reason to persevere when suffering tempts us to question or complain about what God is doing to us.

Chapter 4

Summary of the Guidelines For Interpreting Job

Getting Into the Book

The outline of the book

Before we start reading the long conversation in chapter 3, let's get a bird's-eye view of the book as a whole.

In chapters 1 and 2, God sent suffering into Job's life to prove the sincerity of his love. For a long time, Job endured his suffering in a God-pleasing way. Although he knew God was responsible, he did not sin by questioning God's wisdom.

At the end of chapter 2, Job's three friends came to visit him. They expressed grief over Job's horrible physical condition. For seven days they sat in silence, likely because they didn't know what to say. We are not told the affect their actions of grief or their silence had on Job. But after enduring their silence for seven days, Job found himself forced to speak. His sinless praise of God was interrupted by harsh words of blame.

In chapter 3, Job began to grumble. Earlier his wife had urged him to curse God and die (Job 2:9), but he had refused. Now Job did, in fact, speak a curse. He did not curse God, however. Rather, he cursed the day of his birth.

This complaint provides the springboard for the lengthy exchange that follows between him and his friends. Job wanted to know why God had brought suffering into his life. Job saw no reason for what God was doing to him. Eliphaz, on the other hand, had an answer. He explained that God causes people to suffer because they sin. People should humbly accept suffering as God's punishment for sin, give up their sins, and know that God will take the suffering away.

After Job cursed the day of his birth in chapter 3, there were three rounds of discussion. A friend would speak and Job would reply.

> The first round of discussion (chapters 4–14)
> > Eliphaz—Job (4–7)
> > Bildad—Job (8–10)
> > Zophar—Job (11–14)
> The second round of discussion (chapters 15–21)
> > Eliphaz—Job (15–17)
> > Bildad—Job (18–19)
> > Zophar—Job (20–21)
> The third round of discussion (chapters 22–31)
> > Eliphaz—Job (22–24)
> > Bildad—Job's answer, his final words (25–31)

After the conversation between Job and his friends, a man named Elihu was introduced in a short prose section at the beginning of chapter 32. Elihu was a young man who had listened to the conversation. He was angry at what he had heard. He was angry with Job because "Job had justified himself rather than God" (Job 32:2). He was also angry with the three friends "because they had no answer for Job, but they nevertheless had condemned him" (Job 32:3). Elihu then rebuked Job's friends and gave his answer for why Job was suffering.

Finally, in chapter 38, God began to speak: "Then the Lord responded to Job out of a violent storm" (verse 1). God provided the final word on suffering.

Finally, in chapter 42 after Job repented of questioning God, God vindicated Job's faith and perseverance, rebuked Job's three friends, and restored to Job everything he had taken away.

A Summary of the Guidelines

Let's review the truths we have uncovered in chapters 1, 2, and 42. They serve as guidelines for interpreting the conversation.

Job is a God-fearing man

The book of Job begins with a description of Job's character. Job was described in the loftiest of terms. He was blameless and upright. There was no area of his life that he did not dedicate to God—no part of his life that he reserved for his sinful flesh. He loved, respected, and obeyed God. His goal was to align his life perfectly with God's will. And he shunned everything God considered wrong.

The writer of Job started the book on that note. And twice in chapters 1 and 2, God used the same words to

45

describe Job. In fact, God told Satan that "there is no one like him on the earth" (Job 2:3).

Much of the discussion in the book centers on Job's character. Of special importance is the topic of chastening, introduced by Elihu later in the book. If God is chastening a believer, it implies that the believer has done something for which he or she must be chastened. In Job's case, there was no reason why he should be chastened. In fact, God rebuked Satan for inciting him to send suffering into Job's life "for no reason" (Job 2:3).

It is important to keep this guideline in mind when we hear Job speak about his innocence and decide whether Job was being self-righteous.

Job is a sinner who knows God's forgiveness.

Job offered a sacrifice for his children in case they sinned against God at one of their parties. Job knew God would accept his sacrifice and would forgive his children. This shows that Job understood sin, the need of forgiveness, and, since he couldn't earn forgiveness by himself, his need for a sacrifice. Also, the reason for his sacrifices—that his children might have sinned—shows that he was well aware that all believers have a sinful nature.

Job did not love God solely because God gave him many blessings.

Job was blessed by God and he loved God.

Satan defined the relationship between Job's love and God's blessings like this: Job loves, obeys, and serves God because God has blessed him. If God took away those blessings, Job would stop loving, obeying, and serving him.

God, on the other hand, defined the relationship like this: I have blessed Job with many physical blessings, but he does not love me for that reason. If I take away those blessings, he will continue to love, obey, and serve me.

Job suffered loss and physical pain for one reason: to prove that God was right and that Satan was wrong.

Job's sufferings are sent for no reason other than to prove to Satan that Job truly loved God.

People have given various reasons for why Job suffered. Often, the reasons begin with Satan. Satan wanted to cause Job to suffer and make him give up his faith. In fact, some claim that when Satan was roaming the earth, he saw Job as a prime victim to devour (see 1 Peter 5:8), and when given the opportunity, he asked God's permission to send suffering into Job's life to make him fall.

A careful look at the account, however, has shown that although Satan may have had evil intentions for Job, God was behind what took place in the book, and it was his plan to afflict Job.

God, not Satan, initiated the conversation. God, not Satan, brought up the fact of Job's piety. God, not Satan, laid down a challenge, to which Satan responded with a plan to prove God wrong, and that Job had an insincere health-and-wealth faith.

God wanted to prove that his love and grace means more to believers than all their earthly possessions. Job's perseverance would provide people of all time with an example to follow—an example they *will* follow because they understand the depth of God's love and his salvation in Christ. As we will see, Job questioned God's justice in sending him sufferings. But even Job's complaints never overshadowed or made less significant his faith in God's grace.

Scripture certainly teaches that God, in love, chastens his children to help them put off sin. But the idea that God was chastening Job is completely foreign to God's description of Job and the conversation between God and Satan. We will look at this more closely when we meet Elihu in chapters 32-37.

It is God who brought suffering into Job's life.

As we have said, some say that Satan, not God, was the source of Job's suffering. It was Satan's plan and God played no role other than to set limits to how far Satan could go.

There is nothing in all of Job that says that Satan was ultimately responsible for Job's suffering. Job and everyone else in the book, including Satan and God himself, confessed that *God* was ultimately responsible for Job's suffering and that it was part of his plan.

In fact, why *God* was causing Job to suffer is the subject of discussion throughout the book. Everyone was asking, "Why does *God*, whom we know to be good and gracious, send suffering into people's lives?"

Only if both the suffering person and the Christian comforter know that God is behind suffering can there be a foundation on which Christian support is possible.

Job's friends are not heathen. They are badly mistaken believers.

Job's friends were not evil tools of Satan to deceive Job. They were not demons lurking in the shadows, ready to pounce on him. They were Job's friends, men to whom Job looked for comfort in his affliction. Job, no doubt, thought they were capable of giving him the comfort he yearned for, but he waited in vain for them to give him that comfort.

The friends believed in God, and at the end of the account, God forgave them and restored them to the true faith.

Job is only guilty of one sin: the sin of questioning God's justice.

Before suffering entered his life, Job's life was described in glowing terms. He was an innocent man—not free from sin and without the need for God's forgiveness, but one whose life was completely dedicated to serving God. What is more, during his months of suffering before his friends arrived, Job handled his suffering in a completely God-pleasing way. Twice we are told, "In all this, Job did not sin in what he said" (Job 1:22).

When his sufferings began, Job continued to bless God and was willing to accept whatever God chose to give him. There is no indication that he thought differently until he cursed the day of his birth in chapter 3. After his friends arrived, Job started complaining. Egged on by the false accusations of his friends, Job began to say that God had no right to send suffering into the life of an innocent person like him, and that it was unjust for

God to do that to him. And as we will see, Job considered it wrong for God to hide himself and refuse to give Job the reason for his suffering and a chance to argue his innocence. Again, this was the only sin for which God rebuked Job in chapter 42 and of which Job repented.

Even during the time he is complaining, Job does not stop persevering in faith.

Job committed the sin of challenging God's wisdom and justice. Yet even while he did this, he expressed his faith in God's love. Job's faith, spoken of so highly at the beginning of the book, was not destroyed by his suffering. Job's sinful nature was showing itself when he questioned God. But as a child of God, his new nature remained active. He continued to express his God-given hope and refused to give up his integrity as a servant of God.

In the end, God vindicates his servant Job and blesses him for the rest of his life

God gave Job a blessed end. He replaced everything he had taken away. In fact, he gave Job twice as much as he gave him before. Most important, God vindicated Job in the eyes of those around him. Job became an example and encouragement for all who are suffering because of their faith: "As you know, we count as blessed those who have persevered. You have heard of Job's perseverance and have seen what the Lord finally brought about. The Lord is full of compassion and mercy" (James 5:11 NIV).

These guidelines, revealed in chapters 1,2, and 42, direct

our interpretation of the book of Job and help us speak words of comfort to others in their time of suffering.

~~~~~

Special Topic: Why Do People Suffer? Answers from Scripture

The book of Job addresses the question: How do we analyze what God does in our world, particularly when he sends suffering? It focuses on one special account: that of Job. The account of Job will lead us to God's final answer to that question.

Before we get into the conversation between Job, his three friends, and Elihu, let's look at examples of suffering in the rest of Scripture. We will not be able to look at all the examples. There are many. After all, since the fall into sin, all people experience suffering. But the following list will round out our understanding of suffering and help us evaluate some of the statements in Job in the context of the rest of Scripture. We will see that there are times when God tells us why he sends suffering and times when he doesn't.

Suffering comes into the world

Suffering came into Adam and Eve's life and into the lives of all their descendants (Genesis 3, especially 15–24)

After Adam and Eve sinned, they were afraid of God and tried to hide. God promised to send a Savior to destroy Satan and undo what he had done to them. However, God said that their lives would be filled with suffering.

Sometimes we think that sin inherently affects our bodies and relationships and brings suffering into our lives. No one can deny this. For example, addiction to alcohol or pornography comes with consequences.

But in the case of Adam and Eve, their suffering was not a natural result of what they did. God said that *he* was the source of the suffering they would experience. *He* would create hostility between believers and unbelievers. He would make it difficult for Eve to bear children. He would affect her relationship with her husband. He would curse the ground he had commanded Adam to till. He would cause people to return to the ground from which they were taken. He would drive Adam and Eve out of Eden.

Other than saying that Adam and Eve would die because they ate from the tree of the knowledge of good and evil, God did not specifically say *why* he sent these additional forms of suffering. But God did explain why he drove them out of the Garden of Eden:

> Then the LORD God said, "Behold, the man has become like one of us in knowing good and evil. Now, lest he reach out his hand and take also of the tree of life and eat, and live forever—" therefore the LORD God sent him out from the garden of Eden to work the ground from which he was taken. He drove out the man, and at the east of the garden of Eden he placed the cherubim and a flaming sword that turned every way to guard the way to the tree of life. (Genesis 3:22-24)

God promised to forgive Adam and Eve's sin, but he did not want people to live forever in their sinful condition. He wanted peple to live under the curse he had placed on the world (see Revelation 22:3 in the NIV) and yearn for the day when he would renew the creation, and his creatures would be able to live in Eden again (see Revelation 21 and 22). In light of that promise, suffering helps people yearn for the new heaven and new earth.

Cain's murder of Abel (Genesis 4:1-16)

The hostility between the woman's seed (believers) and Satan's seed (unbelievers) showed itself quickly. Adam and Eve had two children, Cain and Abel. Cain killed Abel. This was more than a sin of human anger. The apostle John explains, "We should not be like Cain, who was of the evil one and murdered his brother. And why did he murder him? Because his own deeds were evil and his brother's righteous" (1 John 3:12). The writer of Hebrews explains this further: "By faith Abel offered to God a more acceptable sacrifice than Cain, through which he was commended as righteous, God commending him by accepting his gifts" (Hebrews 11:4).

This was the beginning of persecution, under which Christians have suffered ever since. Abel suffered because he had access to God by faith and his works were acceptable to him. Believers like Abel anger those who don't share the Christian faith and cannot please God.

But Cain also suffered. God is just and often makes the guilty suffer in this life. Cain experienced God's justice:

> "When you work the ground, it shall no longer yield to you its strength. You shall be a fugitive and a wanderer on the earth." Cain said to the LORD, "My punishment is

greater than I can bear. Behold, you have driven me today away from the ground, and from your face I shall be hidden. I shall be a fugitive and a wanderer on the earth, and whoever finds me will kill me." (Genesis 4:12-14)

Every piece of ground Cain tried to farm refused to return crops. For him, this resulted in a wandering existence filled with hardship and the fear of retaliation.

The flood (Genesis 6-9)

God destroyed the world with a flood. He tells us why:

The LORD saw that the wickedness of man was great in the earth, and that every intention of the thoughts of his heart was only evil continually. And the LORD regretted that he had made man on the earth, and it grieved him to his heart. So the LORD said, "I will blot out man whom I have created from the face of the land, man and animals and creeping things and birds of the heavens, for I am sorry that I have made them." (Genesis 6:5-7)

It is hard to fathom the amount of suffering this caused!

After the flood, God said he would never again use a flood to destroy the world. But natural disasters continue to cause suffering. In the book of Job, Elihu glorified God for his absolute power over the weather. He observed how God uses rain:

The clouds swirl around at his direction.
They do whatever he commands them
over the face of the whole inhabited world.
Whether their purpose is to bring punishment or mercy to the world,
he makes them achieve their goal. (Job 37:12,13)

God gives us rain so we can raise crops. But we also realize the suffering caused by too much or too little rain. Too little and there is famine with its accompanying inequality and strife. Too much and there are floods. And when the clouds "swirl around," it can be God's way of distributing moisture over the earth or his way of sending lightning, hail, tornados, hurricanes, and storms at sea. All people, believers and unbelievers alike, suffer from these and other natural catastrophes like earthquakes and tidal waves.

The unbelieving world suffered in the flood. But the believers Noah and his family also suffered. They experienced the hard labor of building an ark and the terror of experiencing the ark begin to be lifted up by the rising waters. Also, Noah is called "a herald of righteousness" (2 Peter 2:5). As such "he condemned the world and became an heir of the righteousness that comes by faith" (Hebrews 11:7). His condemnation of the world no doubt angered the world—just like Abel angered Cain.

The tower of Babel (Genesis 11:1-9)

After the flood, God commanded Noah's descendants to spread out and repopulate the earth. But people refused to believe that God would protect them if they moved off on their own. So they settled in one place and started to build a large tower. The tower would be a sign of human greatness and a tool to unify them.

So God made the people speak different languages, which made it impossible for them to communicate. He forced them to move away from each other, and he drove them out into the world.

55

Since that time, people have had a hard time communicating with each other. Differences in language, appearance, and outlook have made it impossible for people to unite. Nations and people groups have developed with different physical characteristics and ways of thinking. Because of the sinful human desire to dominate others, people in one part of the world oppress people in another part and seek to control them. This has led to the untold suffering of warfare, slavery, and prejudice.

What people in our sinful world desire is to control: to control God, to control his creation, to control other people, and to control the future. Unbelievers are united in a desire to rid the world of believers, who confess that God is in control of everything. All these sinful efforts at control bring unimaginable suffering into the lives of believers and unbelievers alike. But we must remember that it all started with what God himself did at the tower of Babel.

Israel's rebellion and its result.

Already in Deuteronomy, the Lord warned the Israelites against rejecting him. He told them: "It is the LORD who goes before you. He will be with you; he will not leave you or forsake you. Do not fear or be dismayed" (Deuteronomy 31:8). But if the Israelites were "unmindful of the Rock that bore you, and you forgot the God who gave you birth" (Deuteronomy 32:18), God would send suffering into their lives:

> For a fire is kindled by my anger, and it burns to the
> depths of Sheol, devours the earth and its increase, and
> sets on fire the foundations of the mountains. And I will

56

heap disasters upon them; I will spend my arrows on them; they shall be wasted with hunger, and devoured by plague and poisonous pestilence; I will send the teeth of beasts against them, with the venom of things that crawl in the dust. Outdoors the sword shall bereave, and indoors terror, for young man and woman alike, the nursing child with the man of gray hairs.
(Deuteronomy 32:22-25)

When the Israelites became proud, God would use suffering to humble them.

The final judgment (Matthew 24–25 and throughout Scripture)

God will gather believers and take them into the new heaven and new earth. Unbelievers will see him come but will cry out for someone to help them:

The kings of the earth and the great ones and the generals and the rich and the powerful, and everyone, slave and free, hid themselves in the caves and among the rocks of the mountains, calling to the mountains and rocks, "Fall on us and hide us from the face of him who is seated on the throne, and from the wrath of the Lamb, for the great day of their wrath has come, and who can stand?" (Revelation 6:15-17)

Jesus is clear. An eternity in Hell awaits those who reject him, "where their worm does not die and the fire is not quenched" (Mark 9:48).

In the days before the final judgment, God applies or delays his justice as he chooses. Although people suffer God's anger, God "desires all people to be saved and to come to the knowledge of the truth" (1 Timothy 2:4).

Whether it was bringing suffering into the world and ejecting Adam and Eve from Eden, warning the world against persecution and murder as they watched Cain wander through the world, sending a flood to keep evil from getting out of hand, driving people out of Babel lest their ingenuity create a human-centered world, punishing his people and the other nations for their sinfulness and idolatry, or using his people to proclaim a frightening message that someday he will condemn the wicked—all of this is meant to keep the grace of God's promise from being obliterated by the wickedness of mankind.

Suffering in the lives of Christians

God can send suffering into the lives of Christians for special reasons. Here are some examples from the New Testament.

God can send suffering to warn his people against committing specific sins.

When some people in the Corinthian congregation were misusing the Lord's Supper, God worked to stop them. He also used this as a warning to others. Paul wrote:

> Anyone who eats and drinks without discerning the body eats and drinks judgment on himself. That is why many of you are weak and ill, and some have died. But if we judged ourselves truly, we would not be judged. But when we are judged by the Lord, we are disciplined so that we may not be condemned along with the world.
> (1 Corinthians 11:29-32)

SUMMARY OF THE GUIDELINES

In the early days of the church, a husband and wife, Ananias and Saphira, lied to the Holy Spirit about the size of a gift they had given to the church. God punished their sin with death, which served as a stern warning to the rest of the Church (Acts 5:1-11).

At the same time God can use persecution (which comes on believers because of their faith) as a way of disciplining them because of their own sin or weakness.

The people to whom the book of Hebrews was addressed were in danger of giving up Christ and returning to Moses and the Old Testament Law. In Hebrews 12, the writer points to the persecution they were suffering:

> In your struggle against sin you have not yet resisted to the point of shedding your blood. And have you forgotten the exhortation that addresses you as sons? "My son, do not regard lightly the discipline of the Lord, nor be weary when reproved by him. For the Lord disciplines the one he loves, and chastises every son whom he receives. (Hebrews 12:4-6, referring to Proverbs 3:11,12)

God was using persecution to help them not to give in to the pressure they were under. After talking about how God was using persecution to discipline them, he urged,

> Therefore lift your drooping hands and strengthen your weak knees, and make straight paths for your feet, so that what is lame may not be put out of joint but rather be healed. (Hebrews 12:12,13)

Suffering helps a Christian mature in faith and lead a

God-pleasing life.

Peter described the result of suffering for a Christian like this:

> Since therefore Christ suffered in the flesh, arm your-
> selves with the same way of thinking, for whoever has
> suffered in the flesh has ceased from sin, so as to live
> for the rest of the time in the flesh no longer for human
> passions but for the will of God. (1 Peter 4:1,2)

Paul said that our suffering helps us mature in faith and keeps us focused on our Spirit-given hope in Christ:

> We rejoice in our sufferings, knowing that suffering
> produces endurance, and endurance produces character,
> and character produces hope, and hope does not put us
> to shame, because God's love has been poured into our
> hearts through the Holy Spirit who has been given to us.
> (Romans 5:3-5).

James wrote the same:

> Count it all joy, my brothers, when you meet trials of
> various kinds, for you know that the testing of your faith
> produces steadfastness. And let steadfastness have its full
> effect, that you may be perfect and complete, lacking in
> nothing. (James 1:2-4)

Jesus had all these general reasons in mind when he said to his disciples,

> I am the true vine, and my Father is the vinedresser.
> Every branch in me that does not bear fruit he takes
> away, and every branch that does bear fruit he prunes,
> that it may bear more fruit. (John 15:1,2)

We note that even Jesus, in his state of humility, had to grow like any other human being does. The writer of Hebrews tells us that God made his Son suffer so he could learn obedience to his Father's will. The writer said:

> In the days of his flesh, Jesus offered up prayers and supplications, with loud cries and tears, to him who was able to save him from death, and he was heard because of his reverence. Although he was a son, he learned obedience through what he suffered. (Hebrews 5:7,8)

Sometimes Christians suffer for the sake of others.

Some believers suffer so that God can prepare them to help others. Paul talked about this in his own life. He told the Corinthians:

> Blessed be the God and Father of our Lord Jesus Christ, the Father of mercies and God of all comfort, who comforts us in all our affliction, so that we may be able to comfort those who are in any affliction, with the comfort with which we ourselves are comforted by God. For as we share abundantly in Christ's sufferings, so through Christ we share abundantly in comfort too. If we are afflicted, it is for your comfort and salvation; and if we are comforted, it is for your comfort, which you experience when you patiently endure the same sufferings that we suffer. Our hope for you is unshaken, for we know that as you share in our sufferings, you will also share in our comfort. (2 Corinthians 1:3-7)

In this case, God had a dual purpose for Paul's sufferings. Paul himself experienced God's comfort. In the process, God taught Paul how better to comfort others.

Every Christian who suffers does well to ask, "Perhaps God is preparing me to serve someone he plans to bring into my life."

Suffering for Christ leads to joy given by the Holy Spirit.

Peter said that when our faith is tested by suffering, we are blessed, for we are suffering just like Jesus suffered. As a result, "the Spirit of glory and of God," rests on us, and when he returns, we will "rejoice and be glad":

> Beloved, do not be surprised at the fiery trial when it comes upon you to test you, as though something strange were happening to you. But rejoice insofar as you share Christ's sufferings, that you may also rejoice and be glad when his glory is revealed. If you are insulted for the name of Christ, you are blessed, because the Spirit of glory and of God rests upon you. (1 Peter 4:12-14)

And when Peter and others were beaten by the Jewish leaders in Jerusalem, we are told that they left the council chamber "rejoicing that they were counted worthy to suffer dishonor for the name" (Acts 5:41).

Suffering in the lives of individual believers

Nowhere does Scripture say that every time God sends suffering into a Christian's life, his purpose is to rid that person of a sin or to cause their faith to mature. The most well-known example of this is found in John 9:

> As he passed by, he saw a man blind from birth. And his disciples asked him, "Rabbi, who sinned, this man or his parents, that he was born blind?" Jesus answered, "It was not that this man sinned, or his parents, but that the works of God might be displayed in him." (John 9:1-3)

The disciples were thinking like Job's friends thought, namely, that those who suffer are getting what they deserve. But Jesus specifically says that God caused the man to be born blind so God would be glorified when he healed the man. Could there have been two reasons for the man's suffering, namely, to show God's glory and to discipline the man? In this case, no. Jesus answered the disciple's question by specifically saying that the man was not suffering because of some sin or weakness on his part.

Luke records another example:

> There were some present at that very time who told him about the Galileans whose blood Pilate had mingled with their sacrifices. And he answered them, "Do you think that these Galileans were worse sinners than all the other Galileans, because they suffered in this way? No, I tell you; but unless you repent, you will all likewise perish. Or those eighteen on whom the tower in Siloam fell and killed them: do you think that they were worse offenders than all the others who lived in Jerusalem? No, I tell you; but unless you repent, you will all likewise perish." (Luke 13:1-5)

Here Jesus was responding to the idea that people get what they deserve, like he was in the account of the blind man. In both cases, Jesus said that that idea was wrong. God used the death of some Galileans and some others who lived in Jerusalem to serve as a warning against impenitence and unbelief. These two groups of people were no worse than the people to whom Jesus was speaking.

63

What is more, there is no indication that God used those events to chasten or discipline the people involved. The man's blindness did not serve as God's tool to discipline him but to help the faith of others grow when they saw God heal him. The Galileans who died at Pilate's hand, and the people in Jerusalem who were killed by the tower collapse, were not singled out because of some especially terrible sins they had committed. Rather, their deaths served to warn others against God's quick and final judgment on everyone who does not repent.

In Romans 8. Paul told his readers that they were suffering *because* they confessed Christ: "As it is written, '*For your sake* we are being killed all the day long; we are regarded as sheep to be slaughtered" (Romans 8:36).

Some Christians died for their faith; they became martyrs. *Martyr* means "witness." Martyrdom is the most powerful way Christians can testify to their hope in Christ. It is said that the Church grew through the blood of the martyrs. The unbelieving world looked on as Christians gave up their most precious earthly possession because they knew they have life in heaven—a powerful witness to the hope given by the Gospel.

Peter expressed the goal of persecution a little differently. Christians have "an inheritance that is imperishable, undefiled, and unfading, kept in heaven for you," even though

> now for a little while, if necessary, you have been grieved by various trials, so that the tested genuineness of your faith—more precious than gold that perishes though it is tested by fire—may be found to result in praise and

64

glory and honor at the revelation of Jesus Christ. (1 Peter 1:4,6,7)

At the death of a loved one, we suffer loss in this life. But God looks at Christian death from the standpoint of eternity: "Precious in the sight of the LORD is the death of his saints" (Psalm 116:12-15).

Believers also suffer along with unbelievers from war, natural disasters and man-made catastrophes. One time the Syrians raided Israel. They stole a little Israelite girl from her family and took her back to Syria, where she became a servant in the household of Naaman. She was to play an important role in his life.

> Naaman, commander of the army of the king of Syria, was a great man with his master and in high favor, because by him the LORD had given victory to Syria. He was a mighty man of valor, but he was a leper. Now the Syrians on one of their raids had carried off a little girl from the land of Israel, and she worked in the service of Naaman's wife. She said to her mistress, "Would that my lord [Naaman] were with the prophet who is in Samaria! He would cure him of his leprosy." (2 Kings 5:1-3)

Naaman did go to Elisha, and Elisha healed him.

What suffering the little girl endured! What suffering her parents endured when she was taken away! Why were they all made to suffer? Couldn't God have communicated with Naaman in some other way? One would think so. But that kind of speculation is the first step in questioning God's wisdom.

Consider Daniel. In Babylon, Daniel immediately showed his dedication to God. He fearlessly spoke the truth to the king of Babylon and risked his life for his faith. It is hard to conclude that the suffering of deportation was meant as discipline. All his experiences in Babylon likely resulted in a stronger faith. But it would go beyond what we know of Daniel's life to say that that was the reason why God sent him to Babylon.

Suffering Christians must be approached as individuals. They may even need a different approach at different times. Consider how King David suffered in his early years as he fled from King Saul, who was unjustly trying to kill him. Then think about how God chastened David after he committed adultery with Bathsheba and killed her husband. The reason for the suffering was different in each case.

In all of this, we should never forget that God helps our faith grow in other ways than making us suffer. He also helps our faith grow by showing us his power and mercy. One time Jesus gave Peter a miraculous catch of fish:

> When Simon Peter saw it, he fell down at Jesus' knees, saying, 'Depart from me, for I am a sinful man, O Lord.' For he and all who were with him were astonished at the catch of fish that they had taken" (Luke 5:8,9).

What Christian has not experienced God's power in their life like Peter did and responded with increased devotion to him?

Sometimes God strengthens us by *not* giving us what we deserve. In Romans 2, when Paul was addressing the unbelief of the Jews, he reminded them that they had not experienced some of the horrible judgments God had sent on the Gentiles. Despite the Jews' sins, God had been good to them. Paul told them, "Or do you presume on the riches of his kindness and forbearance and patience, not knowing that God's kindness is meant to lead you to repentance?" (Romans 2:4). What Christian, troubled by a particular sin, has not experienced God's gracious patience and undeserved forbearance, which led them to give up that sin?

We also remember that God "makes his sun rise on the evil and on the good, and sends rain on the just and on the unjust" (Matthew 5:45). In preaching about the sin of idol worship, Paul brought up God's ongoing mercy that was designed to encourage people to search for him. Paul pointed that out to some unbelievers: "He has shown kindness by giving you rain from heaven and crops in their seasons; he provides you with plenty of food and fills your hearts with joy" (Acts 14:17 NIV).

In Scripture God sometimes reveals reasons why he sent suffering into certain people's lives. Sometimes he doesn't, in which cases we are wise not to speculate. We must be careful about how we apply those reasons to the people whom we want to comfort. Although there is much that God reveals to us there is far more that he doesn't.

Part Two: The Conversation

Chapter 5—The Conversation, Part One— Job 3–8 71

Special Topic: The Search for Wisdom to Comfort the
Suffering

**Chapter 6—The Conversation, Part One Continued—
Job 9–14... 103**

Special Topic: The Themes in the Conversation

Chapter 7—The Conversation, Part Two—Job 15–21... 139

Special Topic: God Is Just

Chapter 8—The Conversation, Part Three—Job 22–26. 175

Special Topic: Job's Gospel Hope

Chapter 9—Job's Final Words—Job 27–31 199

Special Topic: Can Christians Appeal to Their Own Righteousness Without Being Work-righteous?

Chapter 10—Elihu Counseled Job—Job 32–37............ 225

Special Topic: Was God Chastening Job?

Chapter 11—God Rebuked Job—Job 38–41 259

Special Topic: God's Wisdom and Power

Chapter 12—Comforting Job 273

Appendix 297

Scripture Index 303

Chapter 5

The Conversation, Part One—Job 3-8

Getting Into the Book

Reading—Chapters 3-8

Job 3—Job's initial complaint

Verses 1-10

> Why was I allowed to be born? If I had died in childbirth, I wouldn't be suffering as I am. May the day of my birth be cursed. May the night of my birth never have been.

Verses 11-19

> If I had died at birth, I would now be lying peacefully in the grave.

Verses 20-26

> I speak for all who are suffering. Why is life given to us only to be spent in misery? Why is life given to people only to have God hedge them in and send terrible sufferings into their lives? I feared such a thing. Now it is happening to me.

Job 4–5—Eliphaz' first speech

Job 4 Verses 1–5

You are so impatient! I'm reluctant to talk with you.

Your counsel has helped many, but when you need help, you won't take your own advice.

Verses 6–11

If you were truly pious, you would be confident. But since you are suffering, we have ample proof that you are not pious. It is a rule of thumb: Evil people are punished by God. They are like lions. As powerful as they are, they are not exempt from God's displeasure.

Verses 12–17

A divine being told me that no one is more just and pure than God. So who are you, Job, to think that you can criticize God for how he is dealing with you?

Verses 18–21

Even the lofty angels know far less than God. If that is so, then what about people like us, who live in flimsy houses, who die and are forgotten, and who quickly pass away without having become truly wise?

Job 5 Verses 1,2

Will anyone agree with the justice of your complaints? Certainly not any of the angels.

Verses 3-5

Only fools become irritated; only fools covet the blessings others have. Fools may seem to prosper, but eventually they are cursed—their homes, their children, their possessions.

Verses 6, 7

Trouble doesn't just happen. People themselves are the cause of their troubles.

Verses 8-16

God is great. He preserves the earth in ways we cannot understand. For example, think of how he sends rain.

God is also just. He foils the plans of the wicked. But he deals justly with believers, which, in turn, gives them hope.

Verses 17-26

Do you want to know why you are suffering? God is correcting you, and for that reason you are blessed. Here's what will happen if you submit to God's will: He will heal your wounds, save you from famine, protect you in battle, and free you from the threats of your enemies. You will never suffer from disaster, famine, or wild animals. Everything will cooperate with you. Your fields will produce. Wild animals will not harm you. Your house and possessions will be secure. You will have many children. You will die in peace.

Verse 27

> We have thought this through carefully. Take it seriously. It is true.

Job 6–7 *Job's response to Eliphaz*

Job 6 *Verses 1-4*

> God has lined up his forces against me, and I am suffering terribly under his hand.

Verses 5-7

> I am complaining because your words give me no satisfaction. They are like tasteless food, which I refuse to eat.

Verses 8-10

> O that God would put me to death right now—before I deny him.

Verses 11-13

> Will I ever recover? No. I've lost all hope of that happening.

Verses 14-21

> Even if I had completely lost faith in God, my friends still ought to comfort me in my suffering. But my friends are like streams that people depend on, but which dry up just when they are needed most.

Verses 22-26

> I have not asked you to do something hard. I have asked only this: Tell me what sins I have committed.

> But you refuse. You see a suffering person, and it shocks you. You hear him complain and judge him

because of the words—the empty words—that his suffering forces out of him. Yet if you tell me the sins for which you are accusing me, I will listen.

Verses 27-30

You are treacherous people. It should be obvious that I'm not lying to you. Please inspect my life, and you will find that I am righteous. I am not lying. I'd know if I were.

Job 7 *Verses 1-6*

The life of a soldier or workman is filled with tedious drudgery. His only hope is a little rest and his daily pay. I, too, eagerly wait for the day to be over so I can rest. But even then, I cannot rest, for my suffering continues through the night. How horribly I suffer! I have no hope that it will ever end.

Verses 7-10

I turn to you, O God. Remember me, for I am but a mortal, a fleeting breath. I will soon leave this world, and no one will remember me.

Verses 11-16

I have no hope, so I might as well complain. God, why do you treat me like a dangerous animal that must be watched and guarded? Why do you frighten me even at night? Just leave me alone. Stop tormenting me and let me die.

Verses 17-21

You are God over all. We are just mortals. Why do you worry so much about us—staring at us every moment?

How do my sins affect you? Are they a burden you must drag around? Why not solve the problem by simply forgiving me. I won't be here forever. My life will soon be over, and you will have lost your chance to show me your love.

Job 8 Bildad's first speech

Verses 1-7

Your words are like empty wind. God is just. When people sin, he punishes them. And that includes your children; they died because they were sinful.

But if you plead with God, change your ways, and approach him with a pure life, he will make you greater than you were before.

Verses 8-10

What I'm saying is the wisdom of our forefathers. We should listen to them, for they are greater than us.

Verses 11-19

Marsh plants will grow if they have water. But without water they wither and die. In the same way, if people forget God, they too wither and die. Without God's blessing, everything on which they lean becomes as fragile as a spider's web. They are like plants growing in a garden and thriving among the rocks. But if they are pulled up, the rocks deny they ever knew them. The only good is that there's an empty spot for another plant to grow.

Verses 20-22

If you repent, God himself will give you true strength and joy. Your enemies will be ashamed and no longer trouble you.

~~~~

Special Topic: The Search for Wisdom to Comfort the Suffering

The debate about true wisdom

The topic around which the book of Job revolves is the search for wisdom to deal with the relationship between God and suffering. Job, of course, was not a heathen. But neither were his friends or Elihu, who appears later in the book. They all believed in the true God and acknowledged that God controls everything that happens on earth. In that respect, they were all on the same page and shared that aspect of true wisdom.

Where they differed, however, was their lack of wisdom about why God was making Job suffer. We, the readers, know that Job was suffering not because his life was sinful but because his life was pious. Much of the conversation stemmed from ignorance of these facts. If Job's friends and Elihu had known what we know, they never would have analyzed Job's sufferings or tried to help him as they did. Nor would Job have accused God of being unjust for making him, an innocent person, suffer.

Yet it had to be this way in order for Job's love for God to be tested. It could not have been a test if Job and his friends had known it was a test. What is more, in order to remain a test, God could not have encouraged Job during the test or answered Job's prayers as he had in the past. The trial was designed to test the sincerity of Job's love for God, which Job had *by faith* in God's Word and promises and not because of the many earthly blessings God had given him.

Because the true reason for Job's suffering was unknown, the door was open to the friends to give Job their wisdom they thought he needed to handle his suffering—wisdom that would direct Job to know why he was suffering so he could do something about it and find relief. Job's friends (and later Elihu) tried to give Job the reason for his suffering. Although Job knew his three friends were wrong, he was at a loss to find the reason himself.

After everyone had wrestled with the question of finding the wisdom Job needed, God revealed to Job the only wise way that he or anyone else must deal with suffering.

Although the debate was harsh and long, the debate, Elihu's speech, and God's final words to Job, enable Christians of all ages to understand the relationship between God, who is in control of all things, and the suffering he sends into their lives and into the lives of those they want to comfort.

In this special topic we will define the wisdom of Job's friends and the effect their wisdom had on Job. This will help us see why their wisdom led to such an intense debate. First, we will quicky describe the wisdom of each of the speakers. This will help us see the big picture.

Job. In the first two chapters of the book of Job, Job responded to his suffering with true wisdom. He acknowledged that God was the source of his suffering, and he knew God's love. He confessed that God had the right to do what he pleased. He did not try to probe God's mind or discover why God had afflicted him. He left his life in God's hands. He continued to praise God and serve him. Job responded twice to his suffering in this way. The writer of Job tells us, "In all this, Job did not sin or blame God" (Job 1:22) and, "In all this, Job did not sin in what he said" (Job 2:10).

If Job had maintained that attitude, everything would have been alright for him. But the wisdom of his friends started to affect him. Job knew that he feared God and had avoided evil all his life, as God had said in the first two chapters. Therefore, he started to conclude that God was acting unjustly toward him.

Job's friends. Their wisdom centered on God's justice. God punishes the wicked and blesses the righteous. Since Job was suffering, they reasoned, he must be a wicked person. They thought that Job should be examining himself to find the sin for which God was afflicting him. And if he ever hoped to regain God's favor and blessing, he should quit committing that sin. They thought that Job wrongly considered himself a righteous person who didn't need God to afflict him. The more Job made that claim, the more strident their words to him became. Finally, because he seemed to be oblivious to their wisdom, they gave up trying to convince him of it.

Elihu. Elihu appeared later in the book, after Job and his friends had ended their conversation. Elihu displayed a God-pleasing understanding of how God often deals with believers, namely, by chastening them. Just like parents discipline their children when they sin, so God disciplines his children when they sin. God's goal in sending suffering is to lead sinners to repent and rest in his forgiveness. Elihu's wisdom was based on what we learn in Scripture. But because Elihu did not know the real reason for Job's suffering, he viewed Job as a believer who had fallen into a sin and was wickedly embracing it. (We will analyze Elihu's wisdom when we look at chapters 32–37.)

God. God's wisdom can be summarized briefly: "When faced with suffering, true wisdom is to trust in God's wisdom." That was Job's wisdom when his suffering began. But under the influence of his friends, Job faltered. He held on to his faith in God's mercy and forgiveness, but he charged God with injustice. For that God rebuked Job and led him back to the wisdom he had at the beginning.

A close look at the false wisdom of Job's friends

The ideas discussed in the conversation are often packed in poetic language and difficult expressions. But when we understand the basic false teaching of Job's friends and how their teaching was leading Job away from God's mercy and into work-righteousness, we will have a good foundation on which to read the book. (Note: To make it easy, we will call Eliphaz, Bildad, and Zophar "Job's friends," even though they mostly opposed him and made his suffering worse.)

We can be certain that the wisdom of the friends was wrong and that it was based on a wrong understanding of how God deals with people. We know this because at the end of the book God told Eliphaz and the other two that they had spoken about him incorrectly and that their wisdom was actually "foolishness" (Job 42:7,8). The friends' misunderstanding of God and suffering drove the conversation. Job spoke in opposition to much of what they said.

So, what is the wisdom of the friends—which no one in the book of Job agreed with, but which is so important for understanding the conversation?

The friends' wisdom can be described by contrasting it with Job's faith and service to God. Job praised God for everything he did. He knew God's love, his promise of a Savior, and his forgiveness. For that reason, Job was content to accept from God suffering as well as blessing and leave himself in God's hands.

The friends, however, approached Job's suffering from a different standpoint. Their starting point was not God's love but God's justice. In his first speech, Eliphaz claimed that God was justly punishing Job for some sin Job was committing, and that if Job repented of that sin and gave it up, God would justly bless him again. The friends made this point in all their speeches.

The friends thought in terms of *retributive justice*, namely, that people get what they deserve. In modern terms, the friends sometimes combined this idea with *restorative justice*, namely that people get what they deserve, but the goal of suffering is not just to punish them, but to restore them so they gave up their sin.

81

Many attribute this idea to people in the ancient world and claim that it was the principle behind all ancient religions. That is likely true. But it was not just a characteristic of people in the ancient world. It's the way people of all ages think. It's natural, human wisdom.

All people know the world was created by God. They know that certain actions are right or wrong, that God is just, and that sin deserves punishment (see Romans 1 and 2). Accordingly, people reason that if they disobey God, the only way to have God's favor is to obey him. All people naturally shape their thoughts—either personally or in their formal religion—around that idea. That was the basic error of the Jewish leaders in Jesus' and Paul's day. Even in Christian circles today, people who confess Christ often overlay their faith with some form of retributive or restorative justice.

To use a doctrinal term, Eliphaz was reasoning on the basis of the *opinio legis*. This is the idea that God rewards or condemns people on the basis of how well they keep his commandments (*opinio* is the Latin word for *idea* or *supposition*; *legis* means "of the law").

Eliphaz began his first speech with this advice:

> Shouldn't your piety give you confidence?
> Don't your blameless ways give you reason to hope?
> Now remember this:
> Who has ever perished if he was innocent?
> Where were the upright ever erased?
> This is what I have observed:
> Those who plow evil and sow trouble will reap the same.
> By the breath of God they perish.

By the blast from his nostrils they come to an end. (Job
4:6-9)

Bildad began his first speech on the same note:

Does God pervert justice?
Does the Almighty pervert what is right?
When your children sinned against him,
he handed them over to the consequences of their rebellion.
But if you will eagerly seek God
and plead for compassion from the Almighty,
if you are pure and upright,
then even now he will rouse himself on your behalf,
and he will restore your rightful dwelling place.
Then, though your beginnings were small,
your final days will be very great! (Job 8:3-7)

Bildad urged Job to ask God to deal with him com-
passionately. But that was immediately followed by the
condition that Job could ask for God's mercy only if he
was already "pure and upright."

Eliphaz also understood something about God's love,
which he factored into his analysis of Job's suffering. We
hear him say in his first speech:

How blessed is the man whom God corrects!
Do not reject the discipline of the Almighty!
For though he may inflict wounds, he also bandages
them.
Though he may strike, his hands also heal. (Job 5:17,18)

However, as with Bildad, Eliphaz did not say that God
wanted Job to repent and find forgiveness. He was
saying that Job was blessed because God was trying to

get him to correct his life. This logic was at the heart of every one of the friends' speeches. In fact, the above references are the only times that the friends specifically said that Job was suffering because God wanted to help him. But even in those cases, their advice on how to regain God's love was based on the *opinio legis*, the idea that God's favor and blessings come by keeping the Law. If Job fully dedicated himself to keeping God's commands, they said, God would bless him.

In Zophar's first speech, we see just how cruel the friends' justice-filled wisdom could be. Zophar went so far as say to Job: "Oh how I wish that God would speak up, open his lips against you, and show you the secret of wisdom. . . . Then you would know that God has even forgotten some of your guilt" (Job 11:5,6).

In his first speech, Eliphaz spoke about people like Job who reject this wisdom:

> From dawn to dusk they are smashed to pieces.
> They perish forever, and no one even notices.
> Won't the ropes that hold up their tents be pulled up,
> so that they die without gaining wisdom? (Job 4:20,21).

Eliphaz was saying that if Job continued on his present course, which was a foolish one, he would die without the wisdom of realizing that he could have given up his sin and altered the course of his life.

Job's friends were not irreligious. They had a deep concern for God. After all, they were the close friends of a man God described as blameless and upright, a man who feared God and shunned evil. But Job's friends were living in a world where God's justice dominated— where people suffered because they were not obeying

God and could end their suffering only by keeping
God's Law. And they were dragging Job into that world.

The danger of the friends' wisdom

The friends' main argument was that God is just and
gives people what they deserve. It is not that they were
wrong on that point, and Job never said they were.
Both Job and his friends would have agreed with Solomon's words: "The way of the LORD is a stronghold to
the blameless, but destruction to evildoers" (Proverbs
10:29), with David's words: "The wicked will not stand
in the judgment, nor sinners in the congregation of the
righteous; for the LORD knows the way of the righteous,
but the way of the wicked will perish" (Psalm 1:5,6),
and with Paul's words in the New Testament: "For the
one who sows to his own flesh will from the flesh reap
corruption, but the one who sows to the Spirit will from
the Spirit reap eternal life" (Galatians 6:8).

Like them, Job knew that God was perfectly just. In his
first speech Bildad said, "Certainly God does not reject a
blameless man" (Job 8:20). Job acknowledged the truth
of that. But Bildad was not speaking about blamelessness as God had spoken about it in chapters 1 and 2.
Bildad was speaking about complete sinlessness, which
forced Job to ask: "But how can a man be justified
before God?" (Job 9:2).

This short sentence explained what Job meant when
he said he was blameless and innocent. Job knew that
his complete devotion to God did not exclude sin
on his part. In view of his suffering, in one place Job
asked God, "Why do you not pardon my offenses and

forgive my sins? (Job 7:13). In Job 9:15, Job said that even though he was innocent, that gave him no right to approach God: "But even if I am in the right, I cannot answer him. I can only plead to my judge for grace." Here Job was saying two things. First, he was in the right. That is, he was faithfully serving God in all areas of his life. Nevertheless, Job knew he was a sinner and could appeal to God only on the basis of God's mercy.

Job also understood something that Paul made clear in the New Testament: Those *who sow to the Spirit* will reap eternal life. He understood that true faith was "of the heart, by the Spirit, not by the written code" as Paul described it in Romans 2:29. The Spirit working in Job came through God's promise of a Savior and from the fact of God's love and forgiveness, not through a list of laws Job was to keep. God's Spirit enabled Job to serve God in all areas of his life without holding back.

The spirit in which the friends urged Job to keep the law was the spirit of work-righteousness. Keep the law because of what you will get by doing so, they said. Job knew that this spirit and the wisdom that came with it were wrong. At the beginning of one of his speeches, he sarcastically said to his friends: "Yes, indeed. You are the people, and wisdom will die with you!" (Job 12:2).

As we will see when we explore the conversation, Job was caught between a rock and a hard place. Actually, there were rocks on all sides of him—all pressing in on his faith. Here is the conundrum Job faced:

• Job knew the friends were wrong. He had never won God's favor by what he did—by work-righteousness.

Nor did he serve God because God had richly blessed him. He served God because he loved him.

• Job also recognized the truth in his friends' wisdom. Job knew there is such a thing as just retribution for sin. God would not allow himself to be mocked by wicked people. At some point God would punish them. But was his own suffering proof that he was a wicked person? That was what his friends contended, and their contention was based on the truth: God *is* perfectly just. Job could not simply dismiss that fact, but he knew there was something wrong with how the friends were applying that to him.

• Each time Job's friends spoke, they accused him of refusing to acknowledge his sins and repent of them. Their proof was the suffering that God had sent into Job's life. Job, however, knew he was a forgiven sinner and that his love for God had led him to live a blameless and innocent life. To go along with his friends and deny his innocence would have been a lie.

• Every time Job said he was innocent, the friends told him that no person is without sin. The friends were right. No one is innocent before God. But Job was also right in claiming to be innocent—innocent in the sense in which God called him innocent in the first two chapters.

• Job wanted God either to vindicate his innocence or tell him how he had sinned. But when Job tried to speak with God, God refused to answer. Through it all, God remained silent and kept on afflicting Job. Job was tempted to conclude that his friends were right, and that God was unjustly angry with him.

• All Job could do was rebuke his friends for their false wisdom. But because he was suffering, his arguments seemed weak. His friends had concrete proof for their wisdom and Job had nothing by which to prove them wrong. In that context, he expressed his frustration with God for not communicating with him and went so far as to accuse God of treating him unjustly and of being arbitrary.

• The friend's wisdom was simple and easy to apply. Job's wisdom was hard to express, especially to people who thought of suffering like his friends did. As the friends again and again accused him of sin, Job was forced to move from one theme to the next in an attempt to sort everything out.

Having no way to prove to his friends that they were wrong, Job did the only thing he could. He rose above human logic and the implications of his suffering and confessed his faith in God's mercy. Amid all the clamor of his friends' false teaching and Job's frustration, Job's confession broke through and gave us a wonderful example of a suffering person who continues to trust in God. It also shows us what gave Job the wisdom by which he spoke correctly about God, as God acknowledged in the last chapter.

But how damaging was the friends' wisdom! They managed to halt Job's simple testimony about God's wisdom and love, which he had twice made before his friends arrived. They led him to replace it with expressions of anger, frustration, and pleas for mercy from his friends and from God.

The friends were threatening to change Job's religion from a "done" religion into a "do" religion. They were influencing Job to evaluate his relationship with God in the context of God's justice rather than in the context of God's mercy. In view of his continued suffering, this tempted Job to conclude that God was no longer forgiving his sins. As quoted previously, he asked God:

> Why have you set me up as your target?
> How have I become a burden to you?
> Why do you not forgive my rebellion?
> Why do you not take away my guilt? (Job 7:20,21)

The friends' wisdom led Job to accuse God of acting wrongly toward him. This error made it impossible for the friends to comfort Job. Theirs was a message of Law—logical, but deadly and disheartening. If Job had not persevered in the knowledge that he, a sinner, had a mediator before God who was arguing on his behalf, his friends' wisdom would have led Job to renounce God.

Job's Wisdom

After much discussion, Job returned to the wisdom that had guided him all his life. Although the friends thought they had wisdom to explain *why* Job was suffering,—after all, their emphasis on justice required that— Job said that since God's mercy predominates what he does, then such "wisdom" cannot be found. The wisdom of God's justice leads to this kind of advice: "If you want God's love and blessing, you must become worthy of it." But the wisdom of God's mercy leads to another kind of advice: "The only true wisdom is to rest in God's promises and to fear the Lord and turn away from evil. And then leave everything else in God's merciful hands."

This was the divine wisdom by which Job had lived. He displayed this wisdom before his friends arrived by continuing to praise and serve God and by not asking the reason for his suffering. Moreover, even when the friends led Job to question God and complain about what God was doing to him, he continued to live wisely and turned away from evil (Job 27:5).

⁓

Looking at Job

The conversation is coherent, but sometimes it doesn't seem to be that way. The friends' point, as we have seen, was easy to understand. But Job had to work hard at expressing why their wisdom was an incorrect way of speaking about God.

To settle the argument regarding Job's suffering, the speakers had to successfully deal with certain subthemes. If the reader of Job can locate the subthemes and understand how they are related to the main point, the conversation can be seen as a unit. We will isolate those subthemes in the special topic of the next chapter. But first, we wll listen to several chapters of the conversation and get a better feel for Job's struggle

Chapter 3 Job wishes he had never been born.

After his friends arrived, they sat with Job for seven days. They were silent because of what they saw. Job described their reaction to his scab-covered body: "Now that is what you are like! You have seen something dreadful and you panic" (Job 6:21).

In a few places Job described his appearance. In Job 19 he says, "I am nothing but skin and bones. I have escaped with the skin of my teeth" (verse 20). In another place he said, "My flesh is clothed with maggots and caked with dirt. My skin scabs over and then oozes again" (Job 7:5). Near the end of the book he says, "My skin turns black and falls off, and my bones burn with fever" (Job 30:30).

He graphically described the affect this had on the people around him:

> He has distanced my brothers far from me,
> and those who know me treat me like a stranger.
> My relatives stay away.
> Even my close friends have forgotten me.
> Even my houseguests and my female servants treat me
> like a stranger.
> They look upon me as a foreigner.
> I summon my servant, but he does not answer,
> even though I beg him to be gracious to me.
> My breath keeps my wife away from me,
> and I am repulsive to my mother's children.
> (Job 19:13-17)

We shouldn't be surprised if Job's friends felt the same way when they first saw him.

Job had to begin the conversation. At this point we should take ourselves out of the role of a scholar trying to analyze the text, and put ourselves in the role of Job's comforter. If his friends had done this, they might have felt more like comforting him.

Job's words are those of a person going through unbearable suffering. Job answered the silence of his friends with a speech in which he expressed the desire never to have been born. He wished God had erased that day from the calendar and silenced the joy of childbirth by closing his mother's womb.

If it was necessary that he be born, Job wished that he had been a stillborn child or that his parents had abandoned him and left him to die. Then he would be at peace in the grave.

Job said he wondered if something like this might someday come into his life. Now it had. He asked God why life is given to those who must spend it suffering, like him.

Already in his first speech, Job began to find fault with God. Each of Job's wishes depended on something only God could have done or that God could do now. He asked, "Why is light given to a man whose path is hidden, to one *whom God has hedged in?*" (Job 3:23). (3:1-26)

Chapters 4–5 *Eliphaz' accusation*

Job's first speech was a desperate cry to God for help in suffering, a wish to be done with life, and a complaint against God. Eliphaz' first speech was a well-thought-out analysis of why Job was suffering and what Job might do to be rid of it.

Little of what Eliphaz said was a direct answer to what Job had said. As the friends sat in silence with Job and after they heard his initial speech, they concluded that Job was harboring sin. They never gave up that opinion, and their concern turned to anger over Job's seeming refusal to listen to them. Job's fate was in his own hands. It would have been impossible for them to comfort him, the friends thought, until he acknowledged that fact.

When Job expressed his wish not to have been born, his friends felt they needed to reply. Clearly, Job was refusing God's attempt to correct him.

Eliphaz spoke first. He reminded Job of the advice Job himself had given to others. Job's advice, Eliphaz said, had strengthened others and raised them up in times of trouble. Eliphaz then accused Job of not following his own advice.

But we ask, did Eliphaz really know how Job advised others? Or was he so deeply entrenched in his own way of thinking that he assumed Job had given others the same advice that he was about to give Job: "Give up your sins, be pious, and then be confident that God will bless you?"

He advised, "Shouldn't your piety give you confidence? Don't your blameless ways give you reason to hope?" (Job 4:6). Eliphaz was not saying that Job *was* pious and upright. He was saying that *if* Job was pious and upright, or if he *became* pious and upright, he could then be confident that God would bless him and remove his suffering.

We must also ask how Eliphaz could have known that Job was not pious? He couldn't have known every detail of Job's life or had the ability to look into his heart. But he didn't need to, so he thought. He knew that Job was not pious simply because God was making him suffer.

He asked Job,

> Who has ever perished if he was innocent?
> Where were the upright ever erased?
> This is what I have observed:
> Those who plow evil and sow trouble will reap the same.
> By the breath of God they perish. (Job 4:7-9)
> (4:1-11)

Throughout the book Job acknowledged his sinful nature, but at the same time he claimed to have given over his life entirely to God. Eliphaz, however, seemed not to understand how a believer could be innocent in his life of service to God but still be a sinner. Eliphaz described an experience he had one night. He saw a vision. In the vision, a form—very frightening—passed before him. It must have been a divine being speaking for God. At least that's what Eliphaz implied. The form spoke ominous words that all suffering people should keep in mind when they evaluate their relationship to God: "And I heard a quiet voice say, 'Can a person be righteous before God? Can a man be pure before his Maker?'" (Job 4:16,17). He applied those words to the angels, "If God does not trust his own servants, if he charges his messengers with error" (Job 4:18), then mankind is even more worthy of God's censure. (4:12-21)

In chapter 5 Eliphaz explained to Job how this applied to him: If Job continued to claim he was sinless, there was no one to side with him. People like Job, who are filled with resentment over their lot in life and whose anger over God's will for them rages with the same force as jealousy—such people will die. They might have a home and raise children, but things will not go well for them. Their children will be destroyed in court by illegal lawsuits, and their wealth will not survive the ravages of thieves. Such problems and punishments are not natural occurrences. They grow out of the foolish actions of human beings. (5:1-7)

Eliphaz advised Job to appeal to God and lay his problem at God's feet. He then spoke a lengthy hymn of praise to God meant to encourage Job. Job's situation might seem hopeless, but God can do all things. (5:8-16)

Eliphaz then brought God's love into the equation. It was one of only two times he and the other two friends would do this. He said that Job's suffering was a blessing from God: "Consider this: How blessed is the man whom God corrects! Do not reject the discipline of the Almighty! For though he may inflict wounds, he also bandages them. Though he may strike, his hands also heal" (Job 5:17,18). (5:17-26)

As we learned from our study of chapter 42, the friends did not speak correctly about God. For this reason, they were not up to the task of speaking about God in a way that gave comfort.

Eliphaz concluded his speech: "Consider this: We have investigated this carefully, and it is true! Pay close attention and apply it to yourself!" (Job 5:27). Eliphaz' solution to Job's problem was simple, but his analysis of God's relation to suffering was superficial. He claimed to have investigated the matter and found his conclusion to be true. Then he blithely commanded Job to think about what he had said and apply it to himself. (5:27)

If you understand what Eliphaz said in this, his first speech, you will understand all the friends' speeches. The friends would bring up a few related points (the subthemes we mentioned above) to underscore their "wisdom," but they lacked any new or more profound thoughts.

Don't expect too much from them. They were like children. Their solution was not new arguments but to repeat their advice' more and more loudly: "You ARE a sinner. God WILL PUNISH YOU until you repent."

This left Job with all the hard work. He had to sort things out. He had to decide whether Eliphaz' words were wise or not. And if not, he had to provide an alternative.

And it is hard work to search for wisdom in such matters. Solomon said, "I devoted myself to study and to explore by wisdom all that is done under heaven. What a heavy burden God has laid on men!" (Ecclesiastes 1:13 NIV84). And concerning Eliphaz's conclusion that the righteous prosper and the wicked are cursed, Solomon wrote, "There is something else meaningless that occurs on earth: righteous men who get what the wicked deserve, and wicked men who get what the righteous deserve. This too, I say, is meaningless" (Ecclesiastes 8:14 NIV84, see also 7:15). Job would ponder the matter more deeply and express his questions and frustrations in much more detail than his friends.

Job knew he was innocent and that his suffering could not be God's attempt to correct him, so he rejected

Eliphaz's advice. Job's seeming lack of repentance made his friends more and more angry and insistent that Job was a sinner. In the first round of speeches, each of the friends tried to encourage Job by telling him about the blessings God would give him if he repented. But in the second round of speeches, there was no reference to promised blessings if Job repented, only talk about the how God punishes the wicked. In the third round of speeches, Eliphaz was the only one who told Job that God would bless him if he repented. Even so, the first part of that speech contains the worst of all the friends' accusations: "Isn't your wickedness great? Isn't your guilt endless?" (Job 22:5), which is followed by a long and explicit list of Job's sins—nothing more than mean-spirited speculation. Bildad's third speech contained no mention of blessings. Zophar had given up and didn't speak at all.

Job 6–7:6 Job pleads with his friends

Job realized that the stress of his suffering was affecting him and that his outburst in chapter 3 was over the top. He apologized for it: "No wonder my words have been rash" (Job 6:3).

They were rash, but didn't his friends understand what horrible suffering can do to a person? Job asked them: "Would I complain if my life were at peace? My outburst shows the horror of my suffering. Like bad food, my life repulses me" (see Job 6:5-7). (6:1-7)

The next set of verses (Job 6:8-13) is a gem. Job had wanted to die to be rid of his suffering. Here he wishes for the same thing but for a different reason. Job felt weak. He felt helpless. In that condition he knew he could easily reject God. So he asked God to keep that from happening. Kill me now, he prayed, "For then I would still have this comfort: Even as I writhe in relentless pain, I have not denied the words of the Holy One" (Job 6:10).

He had two choices: to die or to risk denying God and his Word. He made the choice Jesus wants all Christians to make:

> And [Jesus] said to all, "If anyone would come after me, let him deny himself and take up his cross daily and follow me. For whoever would save his life will lose it, but whoever loses his life for my sake will save it." (Luke 9:23,24). (6:8-13)

Next, Job gave his friends advice all Christians should take to heart: "A despairing person should receive loyalty from his friends, even if he forsakes the fear of the Almighty" (Job 6:14). God does not want us to restrict our comfort to believers. All fellow human beings deserve our comfort in times of suffering, even if they do not believe in God's promises. And even if a suffering believer seems to have given up their faith, one should comfort that person with God's love and try to restore their faith in God's forgiveness. (6:14)

Job called his friends intermittent streams. Travelers arrive looking for water—for themselves and their animals. All they find are dry streambeds. They come for refreshment and must depart as thirsty as they came. Job was like those travelers. He expected comfort from his friends but found none. (6:15-20)

That's all Job wanted from his friends. He had not asked them to pay off a debt or risk their lives in his defense.

All he wanted was their comfort. At the very least, Job said, if they wanted to accuse him of a sin, they should tell him what sin he had committed. It might be hard for him to listen to their explanation, but a clear rebuke has the power to convert, not some vague accusation. But they had nothing to accuse him of, unless they wanted to count the rash words of a suffering man. (6:21-27)

Job urged them to consider him to be a truthful person. If he was a sinner, wouldn't he confess his sins? It was unjust to accuse him of sin. He had always been a righteous person, and he still was. (6:28-30)

Job then rehearsed his sufferings and the affect they were having on his life. He had endured months of futility and nights of agony. "My flesh is clothed with maggots and caked with dirt. My skin scabs over and then oozes again" (Job 7:5).

Some try to identify which modern illness Job might have been suffering from. But perhaps it's best to see his illness as the devil's own brew, some sinister combination of symptoms devised by Satan to bring Job close to death while still keeping him alive (see Job 2:6). Like many—a soldier, a slave, a day laborer—Job was merely living from day to day. He lived without the hope of experiencing anything better. (7:1-6)

Job 7:7-22 Job pleads with God

Job now turned to God.

Recall Job's attitude in the days before his friends arrived. Job continued to trust in God and even to praise him. But the burden of suffering, the burden of friends who gave criticism instead of comfort, the burden of having to maintain his own righteousness, and the burden of being forced to come up with God-pleasing wisdom to explain his suffering—all this started to influence how Job thought about God.

In the rest of chapter 7, Job saw God from two different and conflicting angles. First, Job viewed him as a detective, always lurking in the shadows and peering into every window of his soul. Why would God, Job asked, show so much attention to a weak human being like him? He asked God:

> What is man that you make so much of him,
> that you pay so much attention to him,
> that you inspect him every morning
> and test him every minute?
> Why do you never stop watching me?
> Why don't you leave me alone long enough for me
> to swallow my spit? (Job 7:17-19)

Am I so dangerous, he asked God, that you must send suffering to keep me under control? Am I a great burden you must carry? He sought relief: "I hope that sleep will give me a break from my suffering, but even then, you torment me with nightmares." It was so bad that all he could say to God was "Leave me alone, for my days are just a vanishing vapor" (Job 7:16).

But Job also saw God from a second angle. Job saw God as his friend. He knew God wanted to speak to him like a father wants to speak to his child. But if he died, Job said, God would have a problem. "The eyes that see me now will no longer watch me. Your eyes will look for me, but I will not be there" (Job 7:8). Job ended his prayer as he started it. He knew God loved him, and if God put him to death, he would have lost a chance to affirm his love: "Soon I will lie down in the dust. You will search for me, but I will not be there" (Job 7:21). (7:7-22)

Chapter 8 *Bildad's first speech*

Eliphaz had urged Job to repent. Bildad had listened to Job's response to Eliphaz. He had heard nothing from Job close to a confession of sins or even an acknowledgment that his suffering stemmed from something he had done.

Therefore, Bildad felt he had to repeat what Eliphaz said. Bildad assumed, as did all the friends, that Job's suffering proved he was wicked. Bildad had learned this from the ancients. Past generations of wise people taught that the righteous are blessed and the wicked are condemned. (8:1-19) (The wisdom of the ancients will be another one of the subthemes.)

Bildad encouraged Job with a short list of the blessings he could expect if he repented. (8:20-22)

Chapter 6

The Conversation
Part One Continued—Job 9-14

Getting Into the Book

Introduction to chapters 9 and 10

When you read Job's reply to Bildad in chapters 9 and 10, you find yourself wondering what was going through Job's mind. But it seems that Job himself didn't know what to think. These two chapters bring out the struggle Job was having with the practical results of his friends' work-righteous ideas.

Before he started to suffer, Job lived a blameless and upright life. After God caused him to lose all he owned, he did not give up his blameless and upright life. When his wife questioned why he was still serving God as he had, he rebuked her. When his friends accused him of sin, he refused to admit they were right. Job knew he had not changed, and there was no time in his life that a change in his behavior toward God could have promoted a change in God's behavior toward him.

The friends concluded that since God does not change, Job was the one who must have changed. God is always just. When a person acts righteously, they said, God's justice brings blessings. But when a person commits sin and refuses to repent, God's justice brings suffering.

Job knew that God was just. But since he had not changed, the unchangeable God *had* changed. God had changed from a loving Father, who had showered gifts on his servant, to what seemed to be a tyrant who enjoyed seeing Job suffer. His God of justice had become unjust. Yet Job knew that could not be. So Job was faced with a great problem. That was the problem Job was struggling to understand. And there was no easy way to solve it.

The book of Job is not about Job versus suffering. The book of Job is not about Job versus Satan. The book of Job is not about Job versus God. The book of Job goes deeper. Properly understood, the book of Job is about God versus God. Where can wisdom be found to address the problems caused by the combination of God's love and God's justice when we are thinking about the things that happen in our lives during our time on earth?

Reading—Chapters 9–14

Job 9–10 Job's reply to Bildad

Job 9 Verses 1–4

> I agree. God is completely just. He will punish the wicked and bless the righteous. But how can I, a sinful man, be as just as God? I could never argue against charges God might bring against me. God is

wise and powerful. No one can resist him and come away unharmed.

Verses 5–14

See God's great power! Observe his wisdom! No one can argue with him or question what he is doing. Observe the power of his anger! When he accuses, no one can argue against him.

Verses 15–21

Even if I am right—and I know I am—I still can do nothing other than plead with God for mercy. Yet based on what's happening to me, God's likely response would be to crush me more—and, as with all the sufferings he has sent me, he would be crushing me for no reason. His blows would come fast and furious.

He is almighty and completely just. He is far stronger than me. He alone has the right to hold court.

If I try to prove my innocence, I only succeed in showing that I am a sinner. I can't figure myself out. I know I am blameless, but I still despise myself.

Verses 22–24

This is what I mean when I say that God destroys the blameless and the wicked alike. He laughs at the calamity of the innocent. He is responsible for the evil that comes on a nation. If God is not in control of such things, then who is?

Verses 25–28

My days go by quickly. I cannot just ignore my suffering and pretend that everything is OK. My suffering, which is the evidence of your condemnation, never goes away.

Verses 29-31

If you have already declared me guilty, what good would it do if I tried to live in innocence? No matter how hard I might try, you would still condemn me.

Verses 32-35

How can God and I have a genuine discussion? I am a human being. He is God. No one can bridge the chasm between us and serve as our mediator. My sufferings make me dread God. If God took them away, I could find courage to approach him. But that's not how it is.

Job 10 *Verses 1-3*

My life is miserable, so I won't hold back. What have I done to deserve your condemnation? You created me, but now you reject me. And at the same time, you bless the plans of the wicked. Is that right?

Verses 4-7

Lord, you know I am innocent. But you seem to be searching out my sin and evaluating me like a human being might, quickly and on the surface. But you are not a human being. You know I am innocent. But no one can rescue me from your blows.

Verses 8-14

You have made me. You have preserved me. You have surrounded me with love. But all that time you've been watching for me to sin, knowing that you would not forgive me when I did.

Verses 15-17

Woe to me if I am guilty. But to be innocent is no better. Here I am, humiliated by my shame and misery. If I attempt to rise up against you, you just make my suffering worse. You produce new witnesses to my sin. In anger you marshal new troops against me.

Verses 18-22

Why did you give me life? I wish I had never been born. I wish I had gone straight to the grave. Please leave me alone. Give me a little happiness before I die and enter the darkness of death.

Job 11 *Zophar's first speech*

Verses 1-6

So, I should just sit here and listen to this stuff?

You say, "I am innocent." How I wish God would speak up and make you realize how many of your sins he has forgotten, which by rights you deserve to be punished for.

Verses 7-12

There is no one as perfect as God. If he wants to put you on trial, he knows you are guilty. There is nothing you can say that will change his mind. Nothing you can do to change your sentence.

But why do I bother? It is as impossible for empty-headed people like you to become wise as it is for a horse to give birth to a man.

Verses 13-20

> But if you plead to God for mercy, give up your sins, and live a God-pleasing life, then you will regain your confidence. The memory of your sufferings will fade away. Your hope will be restored, and you will live in joy. Nothing will make you afraid. Unbelievers will watch God bless your act of repentance and realize how little hope they have.

Job 12–14 *Job's response to Zophar*

Job 12 *Verses 1-4*

> What you say is right. I am a sinner. God alone is perfect, and God blesses those who turn to him. But I am innocent of the sins of which you accuse me.

> God used to answer me when I prayed to him. But now, because of my misfortune, I am the butt of jokes and an object of contempt.

Verses 5,6

> The wicked are not punished. They are at peace, and they contemptuously think that suffering is reserved for those less fortunate than they.

Verses 7-10

> God is behind what is happening to me. There is no one else to whom I can complain.

Verses 11-25

> I agree that the ancients have wisdom. And I know that God is perfect in wisdom and controls everything that happens on earth. He blesses, and when he sends judgment on people, no one can stop him.

Job 13 *Verses 1-6*

I agree with some of what you have said. But you misuse these truths and have no idea of how to apply them to my case. In fact, you do more harm than good. Listen now to what I have to say.

Verses 7-12

Will you try to justify what God has done to me by lying about my way of life? Will you flatter God by claiming that he thinks like you, namely, that he gives people what they deserve? On that basis will you serve as his lawyer and argue his case against me? What if God used your criteria to examine you and subjected you to the same line of questioning you are using on me?

Your wise sayings are foolishness. Your speeches say nothing.

Verses 13-19

No matter what God does—even if he kills me—I will continue to present my case to him. And this is no light matter. The fact that I dare come before him and risk my life in the process shows that I am righteous. Otherwise, I would be a fool to approach him and plead my case. But I am righteous, and I trust that he will vindicate me. Prove me wrong if you can, and I will be quiet.

Verses 20-28

God, take this suffering away and let me speak with you. What sins have I committed to deserve this treatment? You treat me like your enemy. I am like a windblown leaf or dry chaff in your hands. You accuse me of sin, and even bring up the sins of my youth. You lock me up and station a guard over me. I sit here and rot.

Job 14 *Verses 1-6*

Everyone's life is short and filled with trouble. We are impure, and no one can change that. But you know that, O God. So why do you keep watching us, intent on bringing into judgment every wrong thing we do? We only have a short time to live. So turn your gaze away from us and let us be. Just let us put in our time and finish our labors.

Verses 7-12

A tree has hope. If it is cut down and receives moisture again, it will come back to life. But our lives are short, and when they are over, we will be no more. We will never live again.

Verses 13-17

Although it sounds impossible, I am confident that I will live again. I will live in the grave until your anger ceases—and it will. And then, at the right time, you will remember me again. Since this is true, I will put up with my sufferings until you change your attitude toward me (like you do when you bring a tree back to life). You will call for me, and I will answer you. Although you keep track of my sins now, someday you will bag up my sins and plaster over my guilt, and I will live in your forgiveness.

Verses 18-22

> Such a time will come. But right now it seems impossible. I am eroding away, and nothing can restore what I have lost. You will consign me once and for all to the grave. There I will grieve for myself alone, unaware of what's going on with those I've left behind.

~~~

Special Topic: The Themes in the Conversation

A summary of the themes

When we read a novel, we expect the plot to track. When we read a non-fiction book, we expect it to present its topic in an orderly way.

On the surface, the book of Job doesn't fit either of those expectations. The friends' main argument, which we described previously, was clear: Job was suffering because he would not give up living a sinful life. Job rejected that idea and argued that they were wrong. But he had no clear and concise answer to give them.

We discussed the general purpose of Job in the previous chapter (chapter 5), namely, to give us wisdom to understand why God does what he does. In this case, why he was making Job suffer.

As we work from speech to speech, we hear Job and his friends branching out into several other topics, or "subthemes." These subthemes might not seem to be connected to each other—a mere series of thoughts that came into their minds. But nothing can be farther from the truth. These subthemes were part and parcel of the search for wisdom. The search for wisdom included successfully treating them.

The subthemes will all come up more than once. If we put ourselves in Job's place or in the place of anyone who is suffering, we realize that often the struggle is not resolved quickly. Things must be discussed more than once and from different angles. The subthemes serve as a skeleton of sorts. Each time a topic comes up, we will have a place to put it, and it will flesh things out. (Note that this gives a repetitive feel to the book of Job, which can't help but be brought over into this present book as the subthemes come up in our treatment of the conversation.)

Here is a summary of the most important subthemes that Job and his friends discussed.

Where can true wisdom be found? The search for wisdom to help the suffering was the subject of the special section of the previous chapter of this book. But a major question in the search for wisdom is: Where can it be found? The friends depended on human wisdom, which they had received from their forefathers. Elihu taught that wisdom comes directly from God when he chastens his people. Job believed that wisdom comes through God's Word. Who was right? This subtheme comes up repeatedly.

Do the wicked always suffer and are the righteous always blessed? Job's friends believed that history shows that the answer is yes. Job claimed that history shows that the answer is no.

Is God really just? This question is at the heart of the book of Job. The friends and Elihu answered yes. The friends claimed that suffering is the result of sin. Elihu claimed that suffering is the tool God uses to chasten believers in love. To Job, however, his innocent life and the suffering God made him endure were contradictory and brought God's justice into question.

If God was unjust, why could Job continue to hope in God?

The friends told Job that if he reformed his life he could again hope in God's favor. Elihu told Job to put his hope in accepting God's chastisement and receiving God's forgiveness.

Job could accept neither of those answers because he knew he was an innocent man. And he knew that his sins were forgiven on account of his Savior.

No matter how much God seemed to have withdrawn from him, no matter how unfair God seemed, no matter that God seemed to have completely changed from what he was like in the days before Job started to suffer, Job would not give up his faith in God's love or his hope for a blessed future. This is what is meant by Job's perseverance.

Perhaps Job's most famous statement is this: "I know that my Redeemer lives" (Job 19:25). And he made more statements like that, scattered here and there throughout the conversation. The hope afforded by the Gospel of God's grace was never far below the surface in Job's part of the conversation.

Related to this was another question: *Why can believers be certain that God is listening?*

113

The friends said that God does not listen to sinners.

Again, Job could not figure out the answer. He was an innocent person to whom God had always listened before. But when Job answered the previous question about why he could hope in God, he was answering this question also. Believers *can* be certain that God is always listening to them.

Can Christians Appeal to Their Righteousness Without Being Work-righteous?

From beginning to end, Job's friends asserted that Job was a wicked person. Job, however, disagreed and said he had lived a righteous life. Was Job right to do that? Some claim that he was being work-righteous. How should we understand Job's appeal to his righteous life?

What impact should God's perfect knowledge and almighty power have on people?

Many of the speeches contain long sections devoted to God's power. However, each speaker had a somewhat different reason for speaking about it.

To the friends, God's power was comforting. Although God punishes the wicked, if the wicked repent, they claimed, God has the power to end their punishment and restore their happiness.

Elihu appealed to God's wisdom and power to support his claim that God was chastening Job. God knew exactly when and how he should chasten a person. When a person repented, God had the power to restore that person to a happy life.

THE CONVERSATION, PART ONE CONTINUED

Job believed that God was all-powerful. He also took comfort in that power. But because God was afflicting him, an innocent person, God's power frightened him. He knew he could not oppose God; he was afraid that God would make him suffer more.

We will expand on the first two subthemes below, and we will cover the other four subthemes in Special Topic sections later in this book.[3]

Where can true wisdom be found?

Along with the search for wisdom to comfort people in times of suffering came the question of where such wisdom can be found. It is easy to get a suffering person to think, "God is making me suffer because I've done something wrong." But it's hard to get suffering people, who knows that God loves them, forgives them, and wants to shower his mercy on them, to say, "God, *who has forgiven me*, is making me suffer."

The friends were confident that their advice to Job was age-old truth. Several times they said that their wisdom came from their forefathers, people much older than them and Job. In his first speech, after laying out his wisdom, Eliphaz urged Job, "Consider this: We have investigated this carefully, and it is true! Pay close attention and apply it to yourself!" (Job 5:27).

---

[3] *God's justice* will be the special topic of chapter 7. *Why could Job continue to hope in God?* will be the special topic of chapter 8. *Can Christians Appeal to Their Righteousness Without Being Work-righteous?* will be the special topic of chapter 9. *What impact should God's perfect knowledge and almighty power have on people?* will be the special topic of chapter 11.

In his second speech, Eliphaz referred to what they had investigated. He asked Job, "What do you know that we do not know as well? . . . The gray-haired and the aged are on our side, men older than your father" (Job 15:9,10).

Bildad said the same:

> Yes, ask the previous generations,
> and consider the discoveries of their fathers,
> because we were born only yesterday and know nothing.
> Our days on earth are nothing but a shadow.
> Aren't our ancestors the ones who should teach you and inform you,
> the ones who brought forth words from their hearts?
> (Job 8:8-10)

According to the friends, the wisdom of the forefathers consisted in a correct understanding of God's justice. In his first speech, Zophar told Job how he could become wise: "Oh how I wish that God would speak up, open his lips against you, and show you the secret of wisdom, . . . Then you would know that God has even forgotten some of your guilt!" (Job 11:5,6).

In his second speech, Zophar appealed to his knowledge of history:

> Don't you know this?
> From ancient times,
> from the time when Adam was placed on the earth,
> the triumphant cry of the wicked has been short-lived,
> and the joy of the godless lasts only a moment.
> (Job 20:4,5).

No doubt, the friends were right. Their wisdom did come from the ancients. However, their wisdom did not come from ancient believers like those listed in Hebrews 11, whose wisdom led them to faith in the Savior.

Elihu said that his wisdom came not from the ancients, but directly from God. He had waited for the old men to speak before he entered the conversation with understanding given to him by God.

> I thought that experience should speak.
> Many years should give a man wisdom.
> However, it is the spirit in a man
> and the breath of the Almighty that give a man understanding. (Job 32:7,8)

He then turned to Job and said:

> Pay attention, Job. Listen to me.
> Be silent, so that I may speak.
> If you have anything to say, answer me.
> Speak up, for I would be delighted to declare you innocent.
> If you have nothing to say, listen to me
> Be silent, so I may teach you wisdom. (Job 33:31-33)

Elihu continued by teaching Job that God was disciplining him. God was speaking to Job through troubling dreams and through suffering, telling him to repent and find God's forgiveness. If Job would but listen, he would possess the wisdom he needed to understand what God was doing by making him suffer.

Job maintained his innocence right up to the end. His words to his friends ended on that note, and he did not bring up the issue again to answer Elihu.

117

Throughout the conversation, Job challenged his friends' wisdom:

> How marvelously you have helped the helpless!
> How wonderfully you have saved the arm that has no strength!
> What great advice you have given to the one who lacks wisdom!
> What great insight you have revealed!
> Who helped you proclaim these words?
> Whose breath came out of your mouth? (Job 26:2-4)

In his frustration, Job could become sarcastic. Once he said, "Yes, indeed. You are the people, and wisdom will die with you! (Job 12:2), and again, "I wish you would shut up completely. For you, that would be wisdom!" (Job 13:5).

Earlier Job had wished to die before his suffering led to a denial of God's Word. We don't know the exact words of God Job was referring to. But from the time of Adam and Eve, God's promise of a Savior was passed down at least by word of mouth. We know this from the fact that there were believers in the world even before Moses started writing down God's words. Job was one of those believers.

On the other hand, the wisdom of the ancients—at least the ancient people Job's friends were referring to—was a heavy burden. It pressed on Job and forced him to ask, "But how can a man be justified before God?" (Job 9:2) and say, "Even if I am in the right, I cannot answer him. I can only plead to my judge for grace." (Job 9:15).

The friends and Elihu thought that a wise person could discover *why* someone is suffering. Job, however, knew that God does not give people wisdom to discover *why* God does what he does. In the middle of chapter 28, Job asked his friends:

> But wisdom—where can it be found?
> Where is the place for understanding?
> Mankind does not know where it is kept.
> It is not found in the land of the living.
> (Job 28:12,13)

The friends depended on the ancient resources they had at their disposal. But Job knew that wisdom which seeks to explain God's just and—at the same time—merciful plans and the reasons behind them cannot be found on earth.

Job said, "God understands the way to it, and he alone knows its place" (Job 28:23). Unless God reveals it to us, there is no way to discover the reason for things like Job's suffering.

The only true wisdom tells how we can serve God:

> . . . saw wisdom and appraised its value.
> He established it and also explored it.
> Then he said to mankind:
> Listen carefully. The fear of the Lord—that is wisdom,
> and to turn away from evil is understanding.
> (Job 28:27,28)

For mankind, the only true wisdom is to fear and love God and to turn away from evil.

Do the wicked always suffer and are the righteous always blessed?

This subtheme is closely related to the search for wisdom and is found throughout the book. There is good reason for this. The friends' argument depended on it.

The friends argued that because Job was suffering, he was among the wicked. To reinforce this argument, they gave descriptions of what *always* happens to the righteous and what *always* happens to the wicked. The key word in their wisdom was *always*. God is *always* just, which means that in this life he *always* deals with the righteous and the wicked in a way consistent with his justice.

Job's counterargument was that even though the wicked are *often* judged and the righteous *often* live in peace, it doesn't always happen that way. "Just look around you," the friends said to Job, "and you will have to agree with us." But when Job looked around him, he saw examples of the wicked living long and happy lives and the righteous being made to suffer.

Job challenged his friends' power of observation:

> Why don't you question those who travel the roads?
> Why don't you acknowledge the lessons they learned?
> They say that the wicked man is spared from the day of
> disaster, and that he escapes the day of raging fury" (Job
> 21:29,30).

Job said nothing other than what Solomon said in Ecclesiastes 7:15, which we quoted previously: "There is a righteous man who perishes in his righteousness, and there is a wicked man who prolongs his life in his evildoing" (Ecclesiastes 7:15) Based on that, he called his friends' argument a "fraud" (Job 21:34).

When you come across this subtheme, realize how important it was. For the friends, their teaching of God's pure justice was at stake. For Job, his right to assert his innocence and to struggle with why he was suffering was also at stake.

When you hear the friends make their argument, you will be inclined to agree with them. That is because they were not wrong. God *is* just. He rewards the righteous and he punishes the wicked.

Earlier we noted a few passages that say this. Here is another. Solomon wrote,

> The LORD'S curse is on the house of the wicked, but he blesses the dwelling of the righteous. Toward the scorners he is scornful, but to the humble he gives favor. The wise will inherit honor, but fools get disgrace. (Proverbs 3:33-35).

From this passage and others like it, one might conclude with Job's friends that Job was a wicked man. But Scripture never forces us to draw that conclusion. When God comes to judge the world, he will treat everyone with perfect justice. However, in this life, things are not that simple. That's because God's mercy—his desire to save all people and keep his children safe—is also at work.

One of the psalmists complained,

> My feet had almost stumbled,
> my steps had nearly slipped.
> For I was envious of the arrogant
> when I saw the prosperity of the wicked.

> For they have no pangs until death;
> their bodies are fat and sleek.
> They are not in trouble as others are;
> they are not stricken like the rest of mankind. (Psalm 73:2-5)

The psalmist continued:

> But when I thought how to understand this,
> it seemed to me a wearisome task,
> until I went into the sanctuary of God;
> then I discerned their end. (Psalm 73:18).

When the psalmist entered God's sanctuary, he saw the matter clearly. He saw it in the context of both God's justice on the wicked and mercy on the righteous.

He came to realize that God had a reason for making the wicked prosperous. He was using their prosperity to set them up for a fall:

> Truly you set them in slippery places;
> you make them fall to ruin.
> How they are destroyed in a moment,
> swept away utterly by terrors!
> Like a dream when one awakes,
> O Lord, when you rouse yourself, you despise them as phantoms. (Psalm 73:19-20)

The Psalmist repented of questioning God's ways and he remembered what he possessed as God's child, a recipient of his mercy. He said,

> When my soul was embittered,
> when I was pricked in heart,
> I was brutish and ignorant;
> I was like a beast toward you.

> Nevertheless, I am continually with you;
> you hold my right hand.
> You guide me with your counsel,
> and afterward you will receive me to glory"
> (Psalm 73:21-24).

Job's friends were living outside the sanctuary and could not find any true wisdom there. Job was living inside the sanctuary where wisdom is found. Unlike the psalmist, Job did not know the reason why God was causing him to suffer. Nevertheless, like the Psalmist, Job knew that he was continually with God and that God was holding his right hand.

Isaiah gave another reason for God's seeming injustice, this time when he causes an innocent person to die. Isaiah wrote:

> The righteous man perishes,
> and no one lays it to heart;
> devout men are taken away,
> while no one understands.
> For the righteous man is taken away from calamity;
> he enters into peace;
> they rest in their beds
> who walk in their uprightness. (Isaiah 57:1,2)

Isaiah and the psalmist experienced situations where God's seeming injustice was actually his mercy at work. Even if we can't see why God does what he does, God has reasons motivated by his grace for why he sends suffering into the lives of righteous people like Job. And he has many reasons, motivated by his absolute justice, for why he does what he does to those who continue to reject him.

Looking at Job

Chapter 9 Job's reply to Bildad

If we look ahead to Zophar's reply in Job 11, we hear what all Job's friends thought about Job's speeches. Zophar began his reply like this:

> Doesn't this *gush of words* call for an answer?
> Can this man's bold talk be justified?
> Should your empty words reduce men to silence?
> Can you be allowed to scoff without anyone putting you in your place? (Job 11:2,3)

We don't agree with what Zophar will say about Job, but there is some truth in his description of how Job replied in chapters 9 and 10. They were, in fact, a "gush of words."

The friends were able to speak in a much more concise, reasoned way. Their wisdom allowed them to do that. But Job's knowledge that he was a sinner, his sense of unworthiness to stand before God, his belief in God's right to judge, his knowledge that in mercy God had always forgiven and blessed him, his experience of God's unprovoked change in how he was treating Job, Job's blameless and upright service to God, Job's sudden losses and unrelenting pain—this confusing mix turned Job's speeches into a jumble.

Job's speeches seem like a jumble to everyone who argues like Job's friends argued. But they do not seem that way to Christians who are going through the same sufferings that Job went through. He sat at home. He looked horrible. Servants and friends had left him. Fools mocked him. Everything he owned was gone. His

Satan-inflicted pain would not subside. He loved the Lord. He was blameless and upright. But he was being treated like God sometimes treats the wicked. He had not changed in his life of service to God. But it did seem as if the One in control of his life *had* changed. Every Christian who experiences extreme pain or loss has felt the same way and knows exactly what Job was struggling with.

Everything Job would say in chapters 9 and 10 stemmed from a horrible situation which ran counter to his logic as a child of God. It seemed to him that the suffering in his life was a testimony against God's grace and forgiveness. Nothing but bare faith, something hidden in his heart and at odds with the clear testimony of his wretched life, could assure him that God's grace was still his.

All of this whirled in Job's mind as he sat suffering. All the while, his friends glared at him for what they thought was his spiritual foolishness and lack of wisdom.

Every time we listen to Job, we must put ourselves in his place. Our task is to evaluate his words, but in order to do that, we must empathize with the confusing situation into which God had put him.

We turn now to Job's response to Bildad and the gush of words that came from his mouth.

What Bildad learned from the ancients was not completely wrong (see what Job said in 9:2). Scripture affirms its truth. God is just. Adam and Eve were driven from the Garden of Eden because they sinned. God cursed Cain because he killed his brother Abel. God sent a flood because people had become evil. God punished the people of Israel when they refused to trust his promises and follow his will.

What Bildad said was no different from what other Bible writers say. We noted some examples previously. Here is yet another. Solomon said that God pays close attention to the sins people commit and treats them accordingly:

> A man's ways are before the eyes of the LORD, and he ponders all his paths. The iniquities of the wicked ensnare him, and he is held fast in the cords of his sin. He dies for lack of discipline, and because of his great folly he is led astray. (Proverbs 5:21-23)

Job never dismissed this truth, and he told Bildad as much. But his thoughts were conflicted. Like his friends, Job was beginning to ask "why." The friends concluded that since God uses suffering to punish the wicked, Job must be wicked. They told him to start earning back God's favor. But he wondered what that meant for a sinner like him. Although he agreed with Bildad that God blesses the righteous, he immediately asked him, "But how can a man be justified before God?" (Job 9:2). Job knew that if God levelled charges against him, he couldn't argue with God. No one can oppose God's wisdom and power (9:3,4). No one can push back against God's charges (9:5-14).

Job wanted to argue with God, but he couldn't. Job knew he had served God faithfully. Even so, he could only ask that God be merciful to him. Even if his arguments were right—that God was oppressing him for no reason—he feared to argue his case with God. Based on how God apparently makes innocent people suffer, all he could expect from God was more of the same. Job said that he did not understand this himself. That is, he knew he had no right to stand before God, but he also knew there was no reason why God should be making him suffer (9:14-21).

Job could only conclude, "'It makes no difference.' Blameless or wicked, he brings them all to the same end" (Job 9:22). God arbitrarily scourges the blameless when he wants. And then he laughs. Job thought about the blind judges who sometimes withhold justice from a land. Job asked, "When a land is handed over to a wicked man, God blinds the eyes of its judges. If he is not the one, then who does it?" (Job 9:24). (9:22-24)

There is no happiness in my life, Job said. One day follows another, and I never know what's going to happen. "If I say, 'I will forget my complaint. I will put on a happy face and smile,'" it did no good. Job would still "dread all my pain, because I know that you will not acquit me" (Job 9:27,28).

He wondered, "Do you want me to work harder? I am innocent; how much more innocent must I become? What is more, you've already found me guilty; what good would it do if I became more blameless? I would be working for nothing." (9:25-31)

Job confessed the great distance between himself and God. There was no one—someone similar enough to the divine God and to human beings like Job—who could bring them both together so Job could present his case without fear. So, Job was consigned to stand in the presence of God alone. (9:32-35) (Note: Here Job was looking for a created being to help him. Later, Job would confess that he did, in fact, have a mediator, God himself, who would come to his aid. [See Job 19:25-27.])

Chapter 10 *Job's reply to Bildad, continued*

Job knew he could not argue his case before God. But in chapter 10, he attempted to do just that. Job was weary of life. How much worse could God make it? So why not just argue his case, which is what he did. (10:1)

Job presented a string of thoughts, beginning with the simple request that God give him the reason for his suffering. He followed that with a somewhat sarcastic accusation: You created me to be your child, but you bless those who spite you. Are you blind? Are you in a rush? No, I know that you see things clearly and that you have plenty of time to investigate everything that happens. You know I am innocent, but still, you trap me in this life of suffering. (10:2-7)

Job reminded God that he made him. He expressed that thought in a winsome way in order to contrast that with what God was doing to him now. He concluded, "You provided me with life and mercy, and your watchful care has guarded my spirit" (Job 10:12).

But there was a nefarious reason behind why God created him. It was so he could watch Job carefully, waiting to see if Job would turn out to be wicked so he could punish him.

But I didn't turn out wicked, Job told God. I am a blameless and upright person. But what difference does that make? You treat me as if I'm wicked. And if

I presume to question your ways, you will come at me with even more sufferings—more witnesses to my guilt. (10:8-17)

All Job wanted was for God to leave him alone. Some day he would go into the darkest place of all, from which there was no return. Before that day came, however, Job pleaded with God to leave him alone and let him have a few days of happiness. (10:18-22)

Job should have rested in God's love for him, as he had in chapters 1 and 2. He should have told his friends that he feared God and shunned evil, that he was blameless and upright, all on account of God's love. He would always praise God. He would never let his sufferings make him question God. That was true wisdom, and Job should have left it at that.

But his speeches became filled with unresolved questions centering on the goal of finding wisdom to understand *why* he was suffering. Job let himself be drawn into the nefarious logic of Eliphaz, Bildad, and Zophar—a logic of truth mixed with error. He also let himself get drawn into various subthemes—topics and questions he thought he had to deal with if he was ever to find comfort.

Looking back at these two chapters, we see the contrast between Job and his friends.

Job had begun to think like some of the ancients to whom his friends appealed, who said that suffering always came to wicked people and good things always came to righteous people. Yet Job also realized the implication of their wisdom. If Job had to work to regain God's favor, the Gospel of God's Savior was

severely compromised and in danger of being lost—
something he would never accept (9:1-3).

The friends had told Job that because God was so powerful, he could regain Job's blessings if he repented. Job
responded that God's power, which was so violently on
display in the sufferings of an innocent man like him,
only made him cower in fear, afraid to approach God.
(9:3-14)

The friends tried to make Job focus on the reason for
what was happening in his life. Job knew he had to
focus on God's grace. (9:14,15).

The friends said that Job's sin had separated him from
God. Job could only respond that God, for some reason,
had separated himself from Job, a sinner but still an
innocent man who served God in every area of his life.
Considering this, he simply could not evaluate himself
and decide what he should do (9:15-21).

The friends told Job that he was suffering because he
was sinful. Job's knowledge of his innocence was forcing
him to conclude that God was arbitrary. (9:22-24).

The friends claimed that Job's suffering was proof of his
sin. Job responded that his suffering was proof of God's
unfair judgment of an innocent man. If God were first
to remove his suffering, then Job would know that God
had not completely condemned him, and he could mus-
ter a bit of courage to approach him (9:25-35).

Job's friends said that if he lived a righteous life,
God would honor that and restore his happiness. Job
responded that if he tried to become more righteous,
God would only expose the filth of his sin (9:29-31).

His friends appealed to their idea that God blesses the innocent and punishes the sinner. Job responded by saying that God was punishing him even though he was innocent (10:1-7).

The friends told Job that if he gave up his sin, he could trust in the greatness and power of God to restore his blessings. Job responded that he could not trust the One who created him only to wait for him to sin so he could punish him (10:8-15).

The friends urged Job to repent and turn to God. Job answered that if he tried to approach God, God would only make him suffer more (10:15-17).

The friends said that if Job gave his whole life to God, God would make him happy again. Job couldn't comply because he had been doing that all along. So he simply asked God to remove his suffering and let him enjoy life a little before he went into the darkness of death (10:18-22).

Job's search for wisdom was complex. His clear understanding of God's grace had come face-to-face with the mysterious ways in which God deals with people in their day-to-day lives—ways that are most often hidden from us.

Under the influence of his friends, Job's simple trust in God's wisdom and grace was being replaced with an anxious and even sinful desire to figure out why God was making him suffer. As we will see, when God finally entered the scene, he had only one thing to say to Job: "I am God, and you are not. Don't try to figure out everything I do."

Chapter 11 *Zophar's first speech*

In the first two verses of his first speech, Zophar gave his analysis of what Job had just said. It was a "gush of words" (Job 11:2). Zophar then bumped the friends' accusation up a notch: "God has even forgotten some of your guilt" (Job 11:6).

Note that Zophar was concerned about making Job wise. He said that God was merely working in tune with the wisdom of the ancients on which he and the other two friends based their advice to Job.

Zophar also brought up the subtheme of God's power and applied that to Job: God had power to do whatever he wished; his knowledge of everything and his perfect justice made him able to deal perfectly with sin and restoration. The truly wise person will understand this. In view of this, Job's gush of words had proved that he had little chance of becoming wise. Job was empty headed, Zophar claimed, and "Before an empty-headed man gets understanding, a wild donkey colt will be born as a man" (Job 11:12). (11:1-12)

After these words of encouragement (sarcastically speaking), Zophar encouraged Job to give up his sin. If he did, God would restore his blessings. (11:13-19) Zophar gave one final warning of what would happen to Job if he remained a wicked man. On that note he ended his speech. (11:20)

Other than being more tactless and judgmental, Zophar said essentially the same as Eliphaz and Bildad.

Chapters 12–14 *Job's response to Zophar and the other friends*

Job began his next speech with a discussion of wisdom. Once again, we see that the entire discussion between Job and his friends revolved around finding wisdom to understand why God was making Job suffer. His friends were teaching him that God is just and that he punishes and rewards people according to their deeds. Again, we see that Job did not dispute that. He asked his friends, "Who doesn't know all these things?" (Job 12:3) (12:1-3)

Job, however, contended that these truths about God's justice were of no help. Why? Because he was "righteous and complete" (Job 12:4). The wicked feel safe, and they scorn people like Job who are going through trouble. We are the ones headed for disaster, they say, not them. (12:4-6)

Here one of the subthemes resurfaces: Does God always bless the righteous and punish the wicked? According to the wisdom of the friends, the answer is yes. Job, however, observed the opposite. Those who serve the Lord are often scorned, while the wicked often live in peace. Job contended that since God is in control of everything, he must be responsible for blessing the wicked. (12:7-10)

Job turned to the ancients. It is true, he said, that they have "listened" to life and "tasted" all that happens. It is true, Job said, that they have accrued wisdom. For that reason, we should honor and listen to them. But they do not have the final word. God does, and people should listen to him first: "But wisdom and power are with God. He gives guidance and understanding" (Job 12:13). (12:11-13)

In the rest of the chapter, Job gave examples of God's unlimited power and the seeming inconsistency of his ways. He notes the variety of people whom the Lord had hedged in. This included not just lowly people but powerful people, not just sinners but "the deceiver *and* the deceived" (Job 12:16).

God controls royal advisors, kings, pillars of society, trusted advisors, elders, and the strong. God can unveil all mysteries, including the mysteries of the grave. God

> raises nations to power, and then he destroys them. He enlarges nations, and then he leads them away captive. He deprives the heads of the peoples of the earth of their reason. . . . He causes them to wander aimlessly like drunks" (Job 12:23-25). (12:14-25)

Job repeated what he said at the beginning of his speech. He, like his friends, had carefully observed life. Their understanding was no greater than his. (13:1,2)

Job knew they were wrong. They had nothing valuable to say. Their words were lies. They were useless, and they should keep their mouths shut. (13:3-5)

The friends had claimed to represent God. They had claimed to know how God deals with sinners, and on that basis they had condemned Job. They were seeking God's favor by arguing God's case for him. But their wisdom about God and his use of suffering was false. Their "axioms are proverbs made of ashes" (Job 13:12). If God examined them, he would censure their lies and false motives like they tried to do against Job on God's

134

behalf. They might fool a person, but they couldn't fool God. (13:6-12)

Jobs friends had warned him against God's judgment. Job told them to be quiet and listen to him. He began with a very reckless statement, but it was a statement whose recklessness was driven by faith. In so many words, Job replied, "I resolve to approach God for an answer. Yes, I know that he condemns sinners, but I also know his mercy and grace. So I will approach him on the basis of his love and not his justice. If he decides to condemn me—even if he kills me—that's OK. It's not going to stop me."

"And by the way," Job added, "my recklessness is proof that I am innocent. Because if I weren't innocent, I wouldn't be stupid enough to approach God"

Job asked his friends to reconsider. If only the friends could list the sins he had committed, he would be quiet and die. (13:13-19)

Job asked God to remove this suffering. Recall once again that before his friends arrived Job praised God in everything. But now Job saw his suffering as a sign of God's displeasure. He argued that if God would but remove his sufferings, that would be proof that God was still gracious to him. Job would no longer be afraid to address God, and a conversation with him could begin. Job would have the courage to ask God to list the sins he had committed for which he deserved to suffer.

Job continued his plea to God in vivid language: "Why do you hide your face? Why do you treat me like your enemy?" (Job 13:24). Job himself suggested the answer: "You write bitter accusations against me, and you hold me accountable for the guilt of my youth" (Job 13:26). The friends' false religion was changing Job. Simple confidence in God's forgiveness was being replaced by questions filled with doubt about whether God really had forgiven him. (13:20-28)

Even though God did not remove his sufferings as he had asked, Job continued his complaint. He expressed a view of human life largely devoid of God's mercy. In one place Job asked God, "You keep your eye on such a man. You bring me into judgment in your presence. Who can produce something pure from something that is impure? No one" (Job 14:3,4). He then asked God to leave him alone. (14:1-6)

Job described the hopeless nature of his life by comparing human beings to trees. When trees are cut down, they only seem to die. There is still life in the roots, and the tree can grow again. But that's not true for human beings. Once they die, they are dead. They have no hope of a pleasant existence. The darkness of temporary life on earth will be replaced by the darkness of eternal death. (14:7-12)

How dreary was Job's description of his life! But faith in God's grace, love, and forgiveness was not dead in Job's heart. Job asked God to let him die, as he did in chapter 3. But here it's not just a request borne of his pain. Rather, Job viewed his time in the grave as a temporary waiting period "until your wrath has passed by" (Job 14:13). Job would wait in the grave until God would "long for the work of your hands" (Job 14:15). Based on God's promise, Job knew that God was a loving Father and that his anger was only temporary.

How beautiful are Job's words at this point:

> Now you count my steps,
> but then you will no longer keep track of my sin.
> My rebellious deeds will be sealed up in a bag,
> and you will plaster over my guilt. (Job 14:16,17)
> (14:13-17)

Nevertheless, Job resumed his hopeless analysis of human life. He accused God: Little by little, with unstoppable power, "you destroy a man's hope" (Job 14:19). Finally, people die. They no longer remember their previous life; they know only the pain of the grave. (14:18-22)

Chapter 7

The Conversation
Part Two—Job 15–21

Getting Into the Book

Reading—Job 15–21

Job 15 *Eliphaz' second speech*

Verses 1-4

> Your words are useless blather. In fact, your claim to be pious only keeps others from finding God and hinders true worship.

Verses 5,6

> The guilt you feel is for the sins you know you are committing. This shapes your arguments, not your fear of God. Your arguments are deceptive. You don't need me to condemn you; your own words do that quite well.

Verses 7–10

> Do you have a corner on wisdom? Hardly. You know
> nothing that we do not know. Plus, the ancient
> fathers are on our side.

Verses 11–13

> Why do you speak as you do? We have brought you
> God's comfort—a sure way out of your suffering.
> But all you do is express your anger against us (and
> against God too) because we have said that your sins
> are the cause of your suffering.

Verses 14–19

> The angels in heaven are not as pure as God. How
> much less pure are human beings. Listen now to
> what I have to say, which is what the most ancient of
> wise men have said.

Verses 20–30

> Look closely at the wicked. Their peace is shattered
> by attackers. They are filled with terror, hopelessness,
> ruin, and hunger. They fear sudden calamity. Why?
> Because they arrogantly rebel against God. They
> may be healthy now, but in time they will live in
> desolate places. They will come to poverty. They will
> die when the hot breath of God blows on them.

Verses 31–35

> What should they do? They should give up pride
> in their possessions. If they don't, God will reward
> them with a useless life. They will try to grow crops,
> but in vain. They will practice bribery, but God will
> punish them for it. They will give birth to nothing

but trouble, disaster, and treachery. This sounds like you, doesn't it?

Job 16–17 *Job's response to Eliphaz*

Job 16 *Verses 1-3*

I've heard all this before. You are miserable comforters.

Verses 4-6

If you were suffering, I could treat you like you're treating me. I could use the same arguments and pontificate about your sins. But I would never do that. I would try to strengthen and comfort you.

If I wanted, I could find things to criticize about your lives and talk about how God is judging you. But I wouldn't do that either. I would give you sympathy and encouragement—like I wish you would give me.

Whether I call to you, God, or not, my suffering continues. You refuse to release me from my suffering. I am convinced that you are angry with me.

Verses 7-18

I am worn out. Just look at my body. All my acquaintances have turned away from me because of how I look. I sense only your hostility and anger. I suffer scorn, contempt, and abuse. God has given me into the hands of the wicked.

I was at ease, but God shattered me. He grabbed me by the neck and tore me from limb to limb. He lined up pitiless archers who shot at me and caused my bodily fluids to spill out on the ground.

He destroyed my defenses and attacked me. I look absolutely terrible.

But I have done nothing wrong, and I can pray to God in good conscience. May the ground that receives my blood never silence my cry of innocence.

Verses 19-21

But I am sure of this: I *will* be heard. I have a witness in heaven. He will testify to the fruits of my faith and will vouch for me. My witness is none other than God himself, and he will plead with God on my behalf. He is my friend and will plead for me like one human being might plead on behalf of another.

Verse 22

Soon I will die.

Job 17 *Verses 1,2*

I will soon die, but until I do, I will have to endure the scorn of those who live around me.

Verse 3

God, when I stand in your courtroom, you will demand me to post bail before the trial begins. But please, I ask, take on that responsibility yourself. You are the only one who can do it and you know I am innocent.

Verses 4,5

You have hidden the truth from the eyes of my accusers. For that reason, they will not win. If they try to use my suffering for their own advancement, even their children will suffer for what they have done.

Verses 6-9

The wicked laugh at me and scorn me. The righteous are appalled at what is happening to me. Yet it will not make them give up their integrity, and they will grow stronger in their resolve not to.

Verses 10-16

So keep trying to find fault with me. But none of you have the wisdom to do that.

My end is near. My plans have failed; my desires will go unfulfilled; I live in darkness. Ahead I see only death and the grave. And all my hopes will descend into the grave along with me.

You promise me hope if I give up my sins—that I will live in the light of God's favor again. But you are wrong. There is no hope for me. Ahead I see only the grave, death, and decay.

Job 18 *Bildad's second speech*

Verses 1-4

Don't treat us like cattle. Come to your senses, and we will get somewhere. The earth isn't going to jump to your ideas.

Verses 5-21

I will show you what will happen if you stay on your present course.

Your light will go out, and you will live in darkness. You will stumble and fall into a net. You will step

into a trap, and you will never get out of it. You will
be harassed by the troubles waiting to devour you.
Disaster will eat your flesh. You will be uprooted and
marched off to death.

None of your possessions will remain. Your property
will lie sterile, and like a tree you will wither and
die. No one will remember you. You will live like
a foreigner and leave no one to take up after you.
The whole world will look with horror at what will
happen to you.

This is the suffering of those who reject God.

Job 19 *Job's response to Bildad*

Verses 1-6

How long will you reproach me with your false
accusations?

Even if you were right and I had sinned, that's
between me and God. You have no right to dig up
my sins and try to put them on display for all to see.
Your only proof is the suffering I am going through.
But know that this is God's doing, unjust as it is.
His will, not some wrong I have committed, is the
reason I am suffering.

Verses 7-20

I cry out to God, who is violently afflicting me. I cry
out to him for help. But I continue to suffer unjustly.

Look at my life. God has taken away my hope. He
attacks me from every direction. He has taken away
my possessions and my honor. He tears me down.
He is angry and treats me like his enemy. He lays

siege works against me. He makes my friends and family despise me. My servants refuse to answer when I call. I am offensive to my wife, sisters, and brothers. Children speak against me. My very closest friends shun me. I have escaped death narrowly by the skin of my teeth.

Verses 21,22

My friends, have mercy on me. The hand of God has struck me. Must you claim that God is punishing me for some sin?

Verses 23-27

Yet I will not give up my hope in God. I will engrave my confidence on stone for future generations to read. I know that my Advocate, my Kinsman-Redeemer lives. He will plead my case. At the end of time, he will stand on the earth. Although my body is destroyed, in this very flesh I will be with him. I will see him with my own eyes. *These eyes* will see him and not those of another! How anxious I am for that day to come.

Verses 28,29

My friends, you insist that my suffering has come because of something I've done. But if you want to see God's righteous judgment in action, you will. If you keep slandering me as you are doing, you will experience his judgment on you.

Job 20 *Zophar's second speech*

Verses 1-3

I feel insulted.

145

You simply don't understand, so let me explain.

Verses 4–28

From the beginning of the world, one principle has always been true: The confidence and joy of the wicked is short lived. Their lofty arrogance will end in a latrine. They are here today, gone tomorrow. Their children must pay back what they took from the poor.

Their youthful vigor will die. They love the taste of evil and savor it as long as they can, but when they finally swallow it, it becomes poison in their stomach. I mean their possessions, which God will make them vomit up.

They will not see good. They struggled to get possessions. But because they stole them from the poor, they will not enjoy them. They want something to eat, but there will be nothing left—their prosperity did not endure. Even when they have what they want, it will soon be taken from them. As they are filling their bellies, God's anger will descend on them, afflicting their very bodies. They flee one weapon only to be struck by another. They pull an arrow out only to inflict on themselves even more harm.

They are terrified. They thought their possessions were safe, but they have been ravaged. A consuming fire will destroy them and everything they own. God will reveal their guilt, and people will attack them. Their house and everything they own will be carried away in a flood on the day of God's wrath.

Verse 29

> What we are saying merely echoes the wisdom of the ages: The joy of the wicked is short lived. You are merely experiencing what all the wicked experience.

Job 21 *Job's response to Zophar*

Verses 1-5

> If you want to comfort me, at least listen to me. But if you will not listen, at least let me have my say. Then go ahead, mock on.

> You wonder why I speak so impatiently. If my complaint were against people, I would be more patient. But it is God, who can look into my heart and see that I love and serve him, who is making me suffer. So why is he treating me like this?! Just look at me. Aren't you shocked by what you see? I tremble at what God is doing to me.

Verses 6-16

> You say that the wicked are always punished. I see just the opposite. Some of them even grow stronger as time goes on. They prosper. They enjoy a happy home life. They have no fear. They celebrate their time on earth. They die in prosperity. When they die, they are spared suffering and pass away quickly.

> All the while they deny their need for God. "We refuse to serve you," they say. "You have nothing to do with our riches and happiness." So why should we pray to you?

> This is the opposite of how I think about God.

Verses 17–21

How often are the wicked actually punished? How often does God give them what they deserve? How often are they quickly removed from their place of prominence?

And you say that their children will pay for their sins, but that's a lame way of looking at it. After all, it's the wicked who deserve to suffer. What do they care about what happens to their offspring after they die?

Verses 22–26

No one can teach God. After all, he rules over the most exalted of people. But it seems as if he deals with people in a completely arbitrary way. Some die having enjoyed a rich and full life. Others die after a life of bitterness. And they both die in the same way.

Verses 27–34

Yet I hear you say, "Prove that to us. We know the homes of the wicked are destroyed."

But that's not true. If you want proof, find some people who have gotten around in the world and ask them what they have seen. They will back me up. Many wicked people go through life without ever being held accountable for their wrongs. For them, death is sweet. They are praised at their funerals, and people even seek to imitate their lives.

My friends, everything you say is wrong. Your advice leads only to confusion and away from God.

Looking at Job

Job 15 Eliphaz' second speech

Like Zophar before him, Eliphaz denounced what Job had just said. Eliphaz asked, "Does a wise man answer with windy bluster?" (Job 15:2), and he followed that up with more derogatory comments about Job's beliefs. Once again, we see that the meaning of wisdom is at issue—wisdom for understanding and dealing with what God sends into one's life. In fact, Eliphaz claimed that Job's brand of wisdom actually kept others from worshipping God in the right way. (15:1-4) Job was speaking as he did, Eliphaz said, because deep down inside, he knew he was guilty.

Eliphaz sarcastically asked Job if he was present when God created the world or if he sat in on God's council meetings. Obviously, not. Therefore, Job was privy to no more knowledge than Eliphaz and the others were.

Once again, Eliphaz emphasized the source of his own wisdom, namely, wisdom passed down from the ancients that had stood the test of time: "The gray-haired and the aged are on our side, men older than your father" (Job 15:10). (15:5-10)

Previously, Eliphaz had told Job how blessed he was to have God discipline him and help him put away his sin (Job 5:17). But Job had rejected this "blessing" by claiming to be innocent. And Job was angry with God for causing an innocent man like him to suffer. (15:11-13)

Eliphaz repeated what he said in his first speech. Next to God, no one is pure, not even the angels in heaven. Much less are mortals. Then in a long and vivid list

of tragedies, Eliphaz described what God does to the
wicked—and that included unrepentant Job. "Before
his time, he will be paid in full.... His grapes will
be shaken from the vine before they are ripe" (Job
15:32,33). This was the wisdom of the ancients, which
the three friends were so proud to know. (15: 14-35)

Job 16-17 Job's response to Eliphaz

The friends had come to comfort Job. But couldn't they
see how little comfort their kind of wisdom gave to
people like Job? (16:1-3)

If the tables were turned and his friends were suffering,
Job said that he could use the wisdom of the ancients
against them too. But Job's wisdom, with God's mercy
at its center, would lead him to do the opposite: "But
instead, I would build you up with the words from my
mouth, and comforting words from my lips would ease
your pain" (Job 16:5).

Job didn't want to answer his three friends. If he did, he
knew they wouldn't comfort him. But he did not want
to remain silent either. Such silence might imply that
they were right and invite even more painful words from
them, miserable comforters that they were. (16:4-6)

Job then turned to God and described what God was
doing to him. Note, here Job moved beyond the actual
pain of suffering. He brought up an even more painful
aspect of his suffering. Job said, "My emaciated body
stands up and is a witness against me" (Job 16:8). My
suffering, Job was saying, is a testimony that for some
reason God is very displeased with me. Physical pain

is not hopeless. However, the pain of guilt is always hopeless.

To better understand Job's pain at this point, contrast it with Job's analysis of his pain in the days before his friends arrived. He said, "The LORD gave and the LORD has taken away. May the name of the LORD be blessed" and, "If we accept the good that comes from God, shouldn't we also accept the bad?" (Job 1:12; 2:10). When Job said that, his pain was no less severe than it was now. But back then his faith completely nullified the pain of God's displeasure. Job rested in God's grace, he trusted in God's love, and his losses and pain were not a witness to the contrary.

However, by the time Job spoke the words of this chapter, the false wisdom of his friends had chipped away at his former trust in God. Now Job was saying things like

His anger has torn me.
He has been hostile to me.
He has gnashed his teeth at me.
My opponent glares at me with piercing eyes. (Job 16:9)

Quite a difference from what he had said previously.

Not only had God sent suffering to Job, God had also sent to Job people who had no ability to comfort him. He said, "God hands me over to evil people. He throws me into the hands of the wicked" (Job 16:11).

Job continued. There was a time when he was "at ease" (Job 16:12), when God was blessing him. But for some reason, that time was over and Job did not know why: "My face is red from my weeping. There are dark circles under my eyes even though there is no violence in my hands, and my prayer is pure" (Job 16:16,17).

Here Job was appealing to his innocence. We will look at this kind of appeal more closely in a later chapter. For now, consider two ways we can understand Job's appeal. Either Job could be appealing to the good things he had done to earn God's favor. Or Job could be appealing to his life of service done because of God's love for him. We will see that he had the second in mind. (16:7-17)

What follows is a beautiful confession of faith. Job knew he had a mediator in heaven, an intercessor who could plead his case with God. The intercessor would not be claiming that Job was worthy of a hearing because he had earned one. Rather, Job's mediator would bear witness that Job's prayer was pure, as was Job's love and service. Job's three earthly friends could never do what Job's mediator would do; their work-righteous wisdom would not allow them to do that.

Job would die soon. May his intercessor act before it was too late! (16:18-22)

Job then rehearsed his desperate condition. He would soon die, but in the meantime, he was forced to listen to the mocking contempt of his enemies (his "friends") who viewed his suffering as a sign of guilt. (17:1,2)

In desperation, Job cried out to God for help. He prayed, "Please pay for me the deposit that you require from me. Indeed, who else could guarantee this payment for me?" (Job 17:3).[4]

[4] Verse 3 literally says, "Place, now. Be surety for me with you. Who is he who strikes my hand?" "Putting up surety" is what we call "posting a bond." Before a trial, if the accused wants to be released from prison before the trial, they must put up money to assure the

Job imagined that he was about to stand trial. In Job's time, like today, an accused person had to post bond before the trial began lest he flee. Job knew he was a sinner and that he could never put up the amount of bail God would require of him. So he asked God, the judge, to be his bondsman and post bail for him. Job was confessing that only God himself could put up the kind of bail money that God himself demanded of a sinner.

All of this makes sense only in the context of Job's wisdom. The Lord would someday pay for the guilt of his sins through the promised Savior. At the present time, Job's suffering seemed to prove that God considered him guilty of committing secret sins. He wanted his day in court to argue otherwise. But to do so he would have to post bail. And he confidently asked God to do this for him because he knew God's mercy and forgiveness. (17:3)

Job denounced the wisdom of his friends. Previously he had asked, "Will you show favoritism on behalf of God and argue his case for him?" (Job 13:8). He was saying the same thing here. By condemning Job in the light of his suffering, the friends had taken the role of prosecuting attorneys, thinking that they were working on God's

---

court that he or she wouldn't flee. The money can belong to the accused, or the accused can try to borrow it from a friend or get it from a professional bondsman. Solomon warned people not to put up surety because of how risky it is: "Whoever puts up security for a stranger will surely suffer harm, but he who hates striking hands in pledge is secure" (Proverbs 11:15). "Striking hands" simply means "shaking on it," making the agreement to put up surety for the accused. Following Job's request that God post bail for him, Job asked. "Who is he who strikes my hand?" Job was saying that no one else could do it for him.

behalf and would be recompensed for their "pious" service.

But they didn't understand the rules of God's courtroom. They considered Job guilty unless he confessed his sin and repented. God, on the other hand, ruled his courtroom with a view to the coming Savior. For believers, God did things in the light of his forgiveness and his recognition that his servants had served him because they knew his mercy.

The friends would be punished for their way of misrepresenting God, Job said. (17:4,5)

With their false system of justice, Job's friends had made him into a laughingstock. This great man was really nothing more than a fraud, they claimed. Nevertheless, there were others like Job, true believers, who realized that the friends were wrong. They shared the wisdom of God, and like Job, would not give up that wisdom in the face of the friends' foolishness. These righteous people "hold tight to their ways, and everyone with clean hands grows stronger" (Job 17:9) That is, the righteous would grow stronger in their own faith as they watched Job persevere.

Job sarcastically waved his finger at his friends, inviting them to try again—to give it their best shot. But he knew they had nothing more to say. Their wisdom had reached a dead end. (17:6-12)

But again, Job's suffering took over and he complained. All his plans—the desires of his heart—had been dashed. Soon he would die. He found no hope in his friends' arguments. He was innocent, but he was suffering under God's hands as a hopeless sinner. And hope does not follow a person into the grave. (17:13-16)

Job 18 Bildad's second speech

To paraphrase Bildad, he asked Job, "Why do you consider yourself alone to be wise and the rest of us to be fools? We are appealing to the wisdom of the ages. Do you think your wisdom can simply dismiss theirs? If so, you are a godless man." (18:1-4,21)

Bildad then launched into a series of short, vivid pictures—one picture per verse—to describe the life of a wicked person. Of course, Bildad was referring to Job. These pictures are easy to understand. One of them must have been especially painful to Job since he had recently lost his ten children. Bildad said that a wicked man "has no posterity or descendants among his people. He leaves no survivor in his place" (Job 18:19). This comment shows how mean-spirited a work-righteous religion can make a person. (18:5-20)

Job 19 Job's response to Bildad

In response to Bildad, Job described what their attack on his faith was doing to him. You "torment my soul," "crush me with words," and "insult me;" you are "treating me so badly." He told them, "You lord it over me." How so? In saying that his suffering was a "disgrace" and was proof of God's displeasure, they had taken the role of his judge. (Job 19:2-6).

But his friends were wrong. He was innocent and therefore not the source of his problems. Rather, God was: "You should know that God has denied me justice, and he has trapped me in his net" (Job 19:6). (19:1-6)

155

Job then described the unjust net in which God had trapped him. Verses 10 and 11 provide a good summary of God's attitude toward Job: "He tears me down on every side, until I am gone. He uproots my hope like a tree. His anger burns against me, and he regards me as his enemy." (19:7-20)

Job yearned for comfort from his friends: "Have mercy on me. Have mercy on me, you friends of mine, because the hand of God has struck me" (Job 19:21). But his friends claimed to be allied with God. Job asked them, "Why do you pursue me the way God does? Will you never get enough of my flesh?" (Job 19:22).

To Job, it seemed as if both the friends and God were following the wisdom of the ancients, which told sinners to forsake sin and become righteous *in order to* find God's love. Job, on the other hand, knew the horror of sin. He had always rested in God's forgiveness, given up the sins for which he had been forgiven, and lived as a servant of God. (19:21,22)

The friends believed that their wisdom was the path to God. Job knew that their wisdom was the path away from God. If Job had denied his innocence, he would also have denied what God's grace had done in his heart. (We will look at this more closely in the Special Topic of Chapter 9, "Can Christians Appeal to Their Right
eous Life Like Job Did?")

In a few verses, Job will express his hope: "I have a Redeemer, and someday I will see him." It might have been good for Job to skip everything he had just said and go directly to that expression of hope. But Job gave into his sinful nature and criticized God for what he was doing. He told Bildad and the others, "You should know that God has denied me justice, and he has trapped me in his net" (Job 19:6). Job was saying that the problem of his suffering did not lie with him but with God: He was innocent and God was treating him unfairly. Before we look at Job's great expression of hope, we will look at what he just said about God's injustice.

Special Topic: God Is Just

Job sinned by saying that God was wrong.

As we have seen, at first Job did not question why God was afflicting him. He simply praised God as he had done all his life and left everything in God's hands. But when his friends taught him that God's justice was absolute, Job began to call God unjust. This was a sin.

How exactly was Job sinning? The answer is found in Job 38–41, where God rebuked Job. There God asked him, "Who is this who spreads darkness over my plans with his ignorant words?" (Job 38:2). Two chapters later, God asked him the same thing, "Will the one who makes charges against the Almighty dare to correct him? The one who accuses God should make his case!" (Job 40:2). God also asked Job, "Will you really deny that I am just? Will you convict me, so that you can be acquitted?" (Job 40:8). He also asked Job, "Who then can stand before me? Who can confront me and demand that I repay him? (Job 41:10-11).

Using these questions we can describe Job's sin. Job spread darkness over God's plans. That is, Job considered God's plans to be coming from Satan's darkness rather than from the light of God's glory. Job said that God was wrong to afflict innocent people. Job thought he knew better and could manage the world more equitably. Job thought that his sense of right and wrong was superior to God's. He thought God should repay him for the harm God's plans had caused. Job's major problem was his ignorance. He did not possess the depth of understanding that God had, so he had no way to evaluate what God was doing to him.

God challenged him to make his case, but Job could not. Already in the middle of God's rebuke, Job spoke up and confessed, "I spoke once, but I cannot defend it. Twice, but I will not go any further" (Job 40:5). When God was finished with his rebuke, Job responded,

> You asked, "Who is this who spreads darkness over my plans with his ignorant words?"
> I have made statements about things I did not understand,
> things too wonderful for me to know. (Job 42:3)

Human beings try to help God by upholding his justice in mistaken ways

When we hear Job say that it was unjust for God to afflict him, believers are quick to label that a sin. And it was. However, we should not be too quick in our evaluation of Job. The matter goes deeper. In fact, the account of Job's suffering leads us into one of the most difficult issues people have wrestled with since the beginning, namely, issues about God's governance of the world and how he directs our lives.

When Job accused God of being unjust, everyone in the book of Job came to God's defense. They thought they could identify why God was afflicting Job. Once they did that, they could dismiss Job's "gush of words," and rest in the conviction that they had successfully come to God's defense.

The book of Job shows us two examples of human efforts to protect God's justice. The friends protected God's justice by saying that Job was a sinner and that it was right for God to punish him. Later in the book of Job, we will watch Elihu protect God's justice by saying that Job was a sinner and that he deserved God's chastisement.

And there are other ways people try to justify God. Some focus on the conversation between God and Satan at the beginning of the book. They say that it was not at all God's plan to afflict Job. It was Satan's plan, and God merely *allowed* him to do that. This somewhat distances God's love for Job from Satan's evil plans for him.

Others might speculate that there are two kinds of justice—one that God applies to us and another that is hidden, which he uses behind the scenes to govern the world. With that thought, Job might have said to God: "I accept your will for me—good or bad—but you must assure me that in some sense you are acting justly."

Still another way to maintain God's justice is to say that mankind, and not God, is responsible for the injustice in this world. It is interesting to note how Job responded to that idea.

Here is why I say, "It makes no difference."
Blameless or wicked, he brings them all to the same end.
If a whip suddenly kills people,
he makes fun of the despair of the innocent.
When a land is handed over to a wicked man,
God blinds the eyes of its judges.
If he is not the one, then who does it? (Job 9:22-24)

Job knew that God was behind everything that happens.
In this case, he said that God is actually behind injustice
in a courtroom.

It is impossible for human reason to prove that God is just.

Here is Job's problem, and the problem faced by every
human being: If there is nothing in a person that has
caused the suffering he is enduring, and if God cannot
be distanced from anything that happens in the world—
particularly the bad things—then what other conclusion
could Job, an innocent man, have come to when he
considered the suffering God had brought into his life?

Was Job correct, therefore, to say that God was acting
unjustly toward him? We tend to answer quickly, "No,
Job was wrong. It was not right for him to call God
unjust." And we do this with good reason. God's Word
tells us that God *is* just. Moses called God "the Rock,
his work is perfect, for all his ways are justice. A God of
faithfulness and without iniquity, just and upright is he"
(Deuteronomy 32:4). The psalmist wrote, "The works of
his hands are faithful and just; all his precepts are trust-
worthy" (Psalm 111:7,8).

Still, there is more to it, and we should explore the matter more closely before we return to Scripture's affirmations of God's justice. Recall the early chapters of Job. Three times we heard that Job was blameless and upright, two times from God himself and once from the author of Job.

Immediately after God said that Job was blameless and upright, Satan picked up the challenge and suggested a plan: "Take away his goods; afflict his body." God then allowed Satan to do as he suggested.

As we have seen, God, not Satan, made Job suffer. God stated this clearly when he described Job's reaction to the first round of his suffering. God told Satan, "He still maintains his integrity, even though you incited me against him to destroy him for no reason" (Job 2:3).

The last phrase in that sentence is significant. God said he destroyed Job "for no reason." Job did nothing to deserve what God did to him.

Compare that with what Job said in Job 9:17. When Job thought about the possibility of getting an audience with God to argue his case, he gave up even before he started. He concluded that such a meeting with God would result in even more suffering. Here is how he put it:

> If I called and he responded to me,
> I do not believe that he would listen to my voice.
> With a violent storm he would crush me,
> and he would inflict many wounds on me *for no reason*.
> (Job 9:16,17)

161

In this verse Job used the same Hebrew word that God used in Job 2:3. God criticized Satan for inciting him to afflict Job *for no reason*. Job criticized God for afflicting him *for no reason*.

So when we hear Job accuse God of afflicting him for no reason, was Job wrong to say that? We must answer, no. If God himself said it, then Job was accurate when he said the same thing.

Here we run into the great challenge with how to interpret the book of Job. On the one hand, Job was correct in saying that God had afflicted him for no reason, implying that God was unjust. On the other hand, from God's rebuke of Job in the final chapters, we know that Job was sinning when he called God unjust.

The question is this: Was God acting unjustly when he destroyed Job for no reason? The question is not a minor one. We spoke about ways people try to disassociate God from the evil that comes into the world. But for anyone who rightly confesses that God is in control of all things—which is what all the people in the book of Job confessed—then the question becomes difficult. And if we rightly disagree with Job's friends who said that people suffer because they are committing sin— then the question jumps out in stark relief.

This is a question everyone has, believers and unbelievers. Is God just when he destroys innocent people for no reason? The unbelieving world says, no, he is not just. This is the chief criticism the unbelieving world levels at God, which they use to dismiss him and even deny that he exists. This question is also at the heart of the struggles Christians have with their own suffering and the suffering of others. And its answer is all important for Christians who want to comfort people in their suffering.

Consider how complex this question is. It is relatively easy to counsel people whose own actions led to their suffering—for example, suffering brought on by a car accident for which they were at fault, or the suffering they must endure because they committed sins that naturally led to a terrible disease.

But even in those situations it is impossible to analyze from the standpoint of justice what God is doing. Even if a person's suffering can be linked to something they did, the basic "why" question still remains unanswered. I might ask myself, "How many times haven't I breathed a sigh of relief when God made me look quickly into my rear-view mirror and I avoided what could have been the same accident as the other person had—even though he or she was keeping their eyes on the road ahead and is suffering for it." Or, "How many times haven't I thanked God for not letting me suffer everything a sinful habit of mine might have caused—the suffering I've watched others endure for the same thing I did? Why did God spare me and not the other person?" No attempt to find a difference between the two of us can make God seem just in both cases.

We have an even greater challenge when called to comfort a person whose suffering had no connection to anything they did. For example, at the death of a baby, even among Christians we hear statements like, "What did the child do to deserve that?" Or consider a young child who suffered from a birth defect for several years before

163

dying a miserable death. Who of us has never thought, "Why did God bring that child into this world? Look at how much they had to suffer, and for what purpose? It's just not fair."

The event could be a natural disaster, a widespread economic catastrophe, or a war. When a tidal wave strikes a beach filled with families or a tornado levels a city, many people endure the same suffering and loss. But the people are very different. Some of those people are living in rebellion against everything they know is right. Others, although they also are unbelievers, are kind to others and live outwardly moral lives. Others might be believers, members of God's family, whose sins are forgiven and are serving God in faith. How do we explain God's justice in such events? Was it fair that any of those people suffered? Was it fair for righteous people to suffer with the unrighteous? And what about the few people who miraculously survived unharmed?

God may be using suffering to lead some of those people to repent. But there is another way he could have done that. In Romans 1, Paul said that God gave some sinners "the due penalty for their error" (Romans 1:27). In Romans 2, however, Paul addressed those who were blindly judging others for committing the very sins they themselves were committing. Paul asked them,

> Do you suppose, O man—you who judge those who practice such things and yet do them yourself—that you will escape the judgment of God? Or do you presume on the riches of his kindness and forbearance and patience, not knowing *that God's kindness is meant to lead you to repentance?* (Romans 2:3,4)

So in some cases God may be leading people to repent by chastening them. But in other cases God may be leading people to repent by pouring out his undeserved kindness on them, patiently withholding the suffering he justly could have brought into their lives. So why does God sometimes use one method and sometimes the other method? This question can be multiplied an infinite number of times in any number of situations.

Thoughts on why God chose Job as the main character of the book

If the book of Job is about how to understand suffering, we might wonder why God chose Job as the main character and the one he made suffer. Why didn't he choose someone more like an average believer?

For example, he could have used David. There were many reasons why David suffered. God described him as "a man after his own heart" (1 Samuel 13:14), but he suffered at the hands of unbelievers. He suffered under Saul because God had chosen him to replace Saul. These sufferings helped him grow spiritually. They gave him a chance to put his full confidence in God, which resulted in psalms of praise for God's deliverance and served as the foundation of his kingship. He also sinned greatly and was chastened by God. He accepted the death of his and Bathsheba's child after he had committed adultery with her and killed her husband. When he was fleeing from his wicked son Absolom, and one of Absolom's allies was pelting him with rocks and cursing him, David accepted that too. He said to his followers, "Leave him alone, and let him curse, for the LORD has told him to" (2 Samuel 16:11). Like God humbled the people at Babel when they proudly built a tower, God humbled David for his pride in counting his fighting men (2 Samuel 24).

In fact, David's life illustrated many of the reasons *why* God sends suffering into the world that we described in the special topic of chapter 4 of this book. If God had used someone like David instead of Job, there would have been many opportunities for the people in the book to discuss the subject of suffering and why it comes.

But why did God choose Job, a blameless man, and then send suffering into his life for no reason?

Consider this simple answer. God chose Job in order to take the question "why" off the table. God's choice of an innocent man to afflict with suffering lead the people in the book to wrestle with the most important question: What should we think when the suffering God sends seems unjust?

Knowing that God is always just is a matter of faith

To ask the question "why," which is what Job's friends forced him to ask, is to enter a world that is infinitely complex and filled with questions that are impossible for us to answer. God gave the readers of the book a rare glimpse into heaven, where we found out why God afflicted Job. But without that information, we could not have begun to understand God's treatment of Job. If we had searched for the reason, we would likely have come up with the same answer Job's friends or Elihu came up with.

But God does not reveal to us what is going on in his mind when he sends suffering–or for that matter, the reasons why he does anything. We dare not speculate about what God has not revealed to us, even if we are trying to protect God's justice.

What God has revealed to us is this: His understanding of the world goes farther than ours. That he understands each individual human mind and heart, that he knows what each person needs, that his afflicting one person may be his way of blessing someone else, that all his plans are just and right as are the goals he wants to accomplish, and finally, that he can see the future and work for the good of his elect—we accept all these things by faith.

Knowing this helps a Christian comfort fellow Christians who are suffering. If a Christian asks what an innocent child did to deserve to suffer, why innocent citizens die in a bombing raid, why natural disasters take the lives of people at random, or even complain that they are undeserving of the suffering that has come into their lives, don't react too strongly. You might say something like this:

> Both of us know that God is in control of all things and that he is just. But I admit, sometimes I feel like you. I think it's wrong for God to afflict innocent people. It seems unjust, and like you, I can't reconcile that with God's love.

167

But there is a book in the Bible that deals with just this question, the book of Job. Job was an innocent man whom God caused to suffer horribly. So what did he do? At first, he accepted the bad things God sent into his life and continued to praise God. But gradually he began to think like we often do: It was wrong for God to do this. He is unfair. He is acting unjustly.

So what did God say to Job? First, he spread before Job the wisdom of his creation and asked Job if he could figure out how he, God, created and governs it. He made Job realize that Job's wisdom did not measure up to his. God was hard on Job, but that's what Job needed. Finally, Job admitted: "I have made statements about things I did not understand, things too wonderful for me to know" (Job 42:3).

Job realized that God can make innocent people like him suffer and still be acting in a just and right way. Like Job, all of us can grow to trust more firmly in the wisdom of God.

People who don't know God's forgiveness in Christ will never be able to accept that God sometimes afflicts the innocent. To know and appreciate God's love for us in Christ is the only thing that removes questions and complaints about God's plans and leads us to accept them. When you meet an unbeliever who challenges God's justice, the best answer is to tell them about your hope in God's grace in Christ. Regardless of how unjust God may seem, he perpetrated the worst unjust act the world has ever seen by telling his innocent Son to suffer the punishment we deserve for our sins.

With Christ's forgiveness in view, we can, in all situations, do what God tells us to do in Jeremiah 9:23,24:

> This is what the LORD says: "Let not the wise man boast of his wisdom or the strong man boast of his strength or the rich man boast of his riches, but let him who boasts boast about this: that he understands and knows me, that I am the LORD, who exercises kindness, justice and righteousness on earth, for in these I delight," declares the LORD. (NIV84)

Human wisdom is a matter of confidence in God's wisdom. We have this confidence through faith in what God says about himself in Scripture and through faith in his promise that all things work for the good of those who love him.

───

Job 19 *Job's response continued*

We have watched Job complain and say that God seemed arbitrary, unfair, and even cruel. Even so, Job persevered in the fact that God is merciful, forgiving, and filled with love for him. This came out most clearly in the next thing he said in response to Bildad.

Job realized that the true God was being replaced in his mind by the false god of his friends. As he had done before, he snapped out of that way of thinking and refused to let it destroy his faith.

He would never deny the truth. He wanted the accusations of his friends exposed for what they were. He wanted his own confession of faith written in stone for all generations to read and confess.

Job had a Redeemer, or Protector. In Hebrew, the word used is *goel* (pronounced go-ale, with the accent on the second syllable). A person in ancient times might have gotten into trouble. They might have sold themselves into slavery to pay a debt. They might have lost their God-given land for some reason. If someone was murdered, a goel was a special relative assigned to avenge that person's blood. A relative was assigned the role of the person's goel and would help that person out of their difficulty.

Job knew he had a Goel. His Goel would protect him from the condemnation of his friends. He would protect him from what seemed to be the condemnation of God himself. Job had said "He regards me as his enemy" (Job 19:11), but his Redeemer would say the opposite, "I regard him as "my servant Job" (Job 1:8).

Job had given up hope that he would be vindicated in his lifetime. After all, God persisted in causing him to suffer, and death seemed imminent. But a time would come when Job would see his Goel and hear him speak up on his behalf. How much he yearned for that day! (19:23-27)

But he was still in the here and now, and his friends were still sitting in front of him. He knew he was right. He also knew that their way of thinking was wrong. If they continued to condemn him, they would merit God's condemnation, and so he warned them: "You should fear the edge of the sword for yourselves!" (Job 19:29). (19:28,29)

***Job 20** Zophar's second speech*

Zophar brushed Job off. Job's confession of a Redeemer and his warning that God would judge them fell on deaf ears. Zophar began, "I heard a rebuke that insults me, so my spirit prompts me to respond with understanding" (Job 20:3). (20:1-3)

What did Zophar understand? He returned to the argument that he and the other friends had been using all along: The wicked suffer, so Job must be wicked.

He referred to the wisdom of the ancients:

> Don't you know this?
> From ancient times,
> from the time when Adam was placed on the earth,
> the triumphant cry of the wicked has been short-lived,
> and the joy of the godless lasts only a moment.
> (Job 20:4,5)

Zophar acknowledged that the wicked sometimes live prosperous lives. But "even when he has plenty, distress catches up with him" (Job 20:22). A wicked person's end comes suddenly, exactly like it had happened to Job. Zophar concluded: "The heavens will uncover his guilt, and the earth will rise up against him. This is God's sentence on the evil man. This is his heritage decreed by God" (Job 20:27,29). (20:4-29)

Job 21 Job's response to Zophar

Zophar said nothing new. Once again, he made the claim that the wicked always get what they have coming—which, according to Zophar, is exactly what Job was getting.

At this point, Job seemed resigned to his friends' indictment. So he told them, "Just listen to me a little more.

171

I know you won't accept what I have to say, but at least it would give me some comfort. After I'm finished, you can continue to call me wicked if you like." (21:1-3)

Job's main problem was with God, not with his friends. "Just look at me," he said to them, "and see the horrible thing God has done. How can you berate me? He is the one responsible for it."

Job was tired of the friends' argument. He temporarily gave up claiming to be innocent, and he began refuting his friends' claim that the wicked are always punished and the righteous are always blessed. What he discovered did, in fact, refute his friends. But his discovery was also frightening to a righteous man like him. If God was arbitrary, then there was the possibility that God might make him suffer more. (21:4-6) (21:4-6)

It was frightening because Job did not always observe wicked people being punished. Nor did he always observe righteous people, like him, being blessed. He described the life of wicked people: They are blessed. They are happy. "They finish out their days in prosperity. Then they go down to the grave in a moment" (Job 21:13). Between life and death there is no intervening period during which they have to suffer. (21:7-13)

Job then related the horrible things the wicked say to God, who had given them their many blessings:

> They say to God, "Keep away from us.
> We know your ways, but we find no pleasure in them."
> "Who is the Almighty, that we should serve him,
> and what benefit do we gain from pleading with him?"
> (Job 21:14,15)

Job assured his friends that he would never think like that. (21:14-16)

Even though the wicked blaspheme God, Job said, God actually protects them! Because of this, some might argue that their children will get the suffering they deserve. But Job said the obvious: "That's not fair." (21:17-21)

Job used this to refute the logic of his friends. If wicked people are often blessed, and innocent people like me often suffer, then you can't accuse me of being wicked based on the fact that I am suffering greatly." (21:22-28)

Job asked them, "Why don't you question those who travel the roads? Why don't you acknowledge the lessons they learned?" (Job 21:29). Travelers can tell you about the many wicked people who have died a peaceful death with long processions following them and holding vigils at their graves.

So don't tell me to change my wicked ways and promise that God will remove my sufferings, Job told them. Considering what actually happens to wicked people, I may as well be a wicked person, as you imagine I am. It makes no difference what kind of person I am. Your wisdom is useless. It is a fraud. (21:29-34)

Chapter 8

The Conversation, Part Three—Job 22–26

Getting Into the Book

Reading—Chapters 22–26

Job 22 *Eliphaz' third speech*

Verses 1–4

> Does God want you to be righteous because your righteousness benefits him? Does he punish you because your wickedness detracts from his bliss? In both cases, the answer is no. He does nothing because of what he might gain from it.

> Another question: Does God make you suffer because you are righteous? Obviously not. That leaves only one reason for your suffering: God is punishing you. And how great your wickedness must be!

Verses 5-11

Let me list what you've been doing. You are forcing your relatives to pay the debts they owe you even though you don't need the money. You take their last piece of clothing. You refuse bread and water to the destitute. You buy up all the land. You refuse to help widows and orphans.

That is why you are suffering.

Verses 12-20

God dwells far above us. But you take that to mean he can't see us and doesn't know what we are doing.

You are doing the same as what the wicked have done from ancient times—people who met an untimely death, whose property was destroyed, who thought of God as useless, and who rejected the fact that he had given them life and everything they own.

I want nothing to do with that way of thinking! We righteous people are glad and mock the wicked because we stand firm and they are cut down.

Verses 21-30

In view of this, put off your wicked ways and be reconciled to God. Do good and shun evil. Then he will build you up. Throw away the gold you treasure so highly, and God will become your gold and silver. You will find pleasure in him. You will look to God, pray to him, and he will answer you. Your plans will succeed. With your help God will save others who are downcast. Because you are pure, he will answer your prayers and release sinners from their troubles.

Job 23–24 *Job's response to Eliphaz*

Job 23 *Verses 1-9*

My suffering is bitter and comes from a spirit weighed down with sorrow. I cannot present my case to God because he is nowhere to be found. I would argue my case with God if only I could find him. Would he reject me? No. He would give me—a righteous man—a hearing. I could argue my case and he would judge me not guilty. But he stays hidden, and I look for him in vain.

Verses 10-12

Nevertheless, God knows that I serve him. No matter how thoroughly he examines me, I will come out with flying colors. I have served him, obeyed his Word, and not turned aside from it. I have rehearsed his commands with my lips and treasured them in my heart.

Verses 13-17

But he stands aloof, and I cannot reach him. He carries out his decrees against me, and how many of them there are! I am in a panic. I have lost all heart. I am terrified of him.

Nevertheless, even though God hides in darkness, I will continue to lay my case before him.

Job 24 *Verses 1-12*

Why doesn't God hold court for the oppressed? Think of the many in this world who suffer injustice from the wicked. They groan every day. The wicked steal their property, flocks, and donkeys. They take the widow's ox as collateral on a loan.

The poor are cast off; they go out into the wilderness looking for some straw to eat. They rely on gleanings from the wicked man's grapevines. At night they lie in the cold without clothing or cover. They cling to cliffs to avoid the heavy mountain rains. The wicked even take their nursing children for collateral.

The poor have little clothing. They do the work of harvesting the grain but have nothing to eat. They pull the stone that crushes the olives. They tread the grapes in the winepress, but they are forbidden to drink. They cry out for help in their misery, but God does not charge the wicked with wrongdoing.

Verses 13-17

Look! The wicked do their work at night when no one can see them. The murderer kills and robs the poor. The adulterer sneaks around in the darkness with covered face. During the daylight hours, they shut themselves indoors lest they be seen.

Verses 18-25

Don't think that I disagree with you about the fact that God punishes wicked people. I do not deny that a wicked person does not succeed. He is aimless. His land is cursed. No one buys his produce. He melts into the grave. His mother forgets him, and the worms eat him. He is cut down like a tree.

He preys on the childless woman and ignores the widow. God drags him away. He gives him security and success for a while, but he is always watching him. Finally, the wicked are cut down in death like the rest of mankind.

So don't think that I deny what happens to the wicked just to protect myself because God is afflicting me.

Job 25 *Bildad's third speech*

Verses 1-3

God is great and rules over all things on earth and in heaven. Who can understand his power?

Verses 4-6

How can anyone claim to be pure? The brightness of the moon and stars is dim compared with him. And sinful mankind has less light than either of them.

Job 26 *Job's answer to Bildad*

Verses 1-4

How wise are your words! How much they help the weak and powerless! How insightful they are to those looking for wisdom!

What spirit gave you such understanding? It certainly wasn't the Spirit of God.

Verses 5-14

Look at God's power. He understands death and knows what happens in the grave. He created the heavens and the earth. He created the rain, storing it in something as light as the clouds. He separated darkness from light. He supports the heavens above the earth. He calms the sea and makes the heavens beautiful. He destroys the forces of evil.

And that is just the beginning of his wisdom and power. Who understands the thunder, I might add?

Looking at Job

Job 22 *Eliphaz' third speech*

Job had claimed repeatedly that he was a righteous person. Eliphaz evidently thought that Job claimed that his righteous life merited something from God and that God should never have made him suffer. Eliphaz commented on this: Job was suffering, but it's not because he was righteous. (22:1-4)

Eliphaz then returned to the argument of his first speech: Job was suffering because of a sin of which he refused to repent.

After Job's refusal to acknowledge that he was a sinner, Eliphaz became much harsher on Job than he had been in his first speech. He came up with a whole list of sins Job had committed. He introduced his list with these words: "Isn't your wickedness great? Isn't your guilt endless?" (Job 22:5). Eliphaz' list was pure, mean-spirited speculation. Once again, we see how far the friends were willing to go to protect their false wisdom about God's absolute justice. (22:5-11)

At the end of his speech. Eliphaz twisted Job's words. Job had said that God, who had once guided and guarded his life as his close friend, had now hidden himself and refused to speak with Job and even seemed to be unaware of what was happening to him. Job had supposedly claimed that between human beings and God there is a dark cloud that God's eyes cannot penetrate. Eliphaz disagreed and said that God sees all things.

Eliphaz accused Job of thinking like wicked people have always thought. Although the wicked should have confessed that God was the source of their blessings, they pushed him away. Consequently, God punished them by ending their lives before their time.

Eliphaz rejected Job's claim that God sends bad things into the lives of both the righteous and the wicked. No, he claimed, God brings suffering only into the lives of the wicked. That helps the righteous understand the nature of wickedness and avoid it. They are encouraged to know that their oppressors will get what they have coming. (22:12-20)

Because of Job's continued affirmation of his innocence, Eliphaz no longer saw Job as a believer who was committing a sin for which God was disciplining him. He encouraged Job to *return* to God:

> Be reconciled with God.
> Be at peace with him.
> Then good will come to you.
> Accept teaching from his mouth,
> and set his words in your heart. (Job 22:21,22).

He promised Job:

> Throw your purest gold into the dust
> and your gold from Ophir upon the rocks in the ravines.
> Then the Almighty will be your purest gold
> and your most precious silver. (Job 22:24,25)

How ironic this was. At the very moment when God was using Job's suffering to prove to Satan that he, the

Almighty, was Job's purest gold, Eliphaz was using Job's suffering to prove that Job valued money more than he valued God. Eliphaz' human wisdom was challenging Job's God-given wisdom. Would Job persevere?

(22:21-30)

Job 23–24 *Job's response to Eliphaz*

According to Eliphaz, Job didn't think that God could see him. We see that Eliphaz was wrong. Job did not deny that God could see *him*. The problem was that Job couldn't find God: "I wish I knew where I could find him, so that I could come to his place for judgment. Then I would lay out my case before him" (Job 23:3,4).

Job was confident that God would find him innocent: "Would he use his great power to press charges against me? He will certainly give me a hearing. There, an upright man could argue with him, and I would be delivered from my judge forever" (Job 23:6,7). Job was right. Job did not serve God to earn God's blessings. He served God because he honored, respected, and loved God. He was confident that God would say to him, "Well done, good and faithful servant. You have been faithful over a little; I will set you over much. Enter into the joy of your master" (Matthew 25:21).

Before Job began to suffer, he experienced God's power at work, richly blessing him and guarding him against harm. Without ceasing to serve God—and with no intent of doing so—Job was now experiencing God's power to destroy. Job could not understand God's present use of his power, and he was frustrated even to the point of accusing God of injustice—to the point of feeling bitter and rebellious toward God,[5] as he said in verse 2.

But Job would never give up his hope, which was based on the Gospel of God's forgiveness. He said, "Would he use his great power to press charges against me? No, he will certainly give me a hearing" (Job 23:6). When Job felt anger over how God was treating him, he always restated his confidence in God's grace (which had inspired his life of innocence): "There, an upright man could argue with him, and I would be delivered from my judge forever" (Job 23:7). Only forgiven sinners can be sure that God will allow them to argue with him and not face his judgment on earth or in eternity. (23:1-7)

But no matter where he turned, Job could not find God. Nevertheless, this did not cause him to doubt God's love for him. Job might not be able to find God, but God saw him and knew everything about him. Job again appealed to his faith-generated life of service: "But I am sure he knows the way I take. When he has tested me, I will come out like gold" (Job 23:10). God could look into every corner of his life and find dedication and service. He was indeed blameless and upright as God had said repeatedly in the beginning of the book. He was confident that when God was finished examining him, he would give Job a gold star. (23:8-12)

After that beautiful statement of faith by one who had been made new through God's grace, Job's sinful nature plagued him again. Job mourned, "God has made me lose heart. The Almighty has terrified me" (Job 23:16). For several verses, Job's sinful nature had its way. But in

[5] See the note on this verse in the EHV version. We are combining both of the options they note.

the last verse of this section, Job showed which voice—
that of his new man or that of the old—would have the
final word: "Nevertheless, I am not silenced by the darkness, by the dark cloud that covers my face" (Job 23:17).
Things were dark on Job's side. But Job knew that things
were still bright on God's side. (23:13-17)

Job returned to the theme of justice. This part of Job's
reply to Eliphas is relatively easy to understand.

Job introduced his topic by saying, "Why are appoint-
ments never scheduled by the Almighty? Why do those
who know him never see such days?" (Job 24:1). Here
Job's request is general. He wanted to know why God
does not give a hearing to all righteous people who are
suffering at the hands of the wicked.

The wicked oppress the righteous in any number of
ways. (24:2-4,9,21) They are murderers, adulterers, and
thieves. They work under the cover of darkness. They
hide in the daytime lest they be exposed. (24:13-17) So
the righteous must suffer. (24:5-8;10-12)

Job complained: "Wounded souls cry out for help, but
God does not bring charges against anyone" (Job 24:12).
But although the wicked appear to have everything,
in various ways God will give them what their deeds
deserve. It may take a while for this to happen, but God
will make it happen. (24:22-24)

The friends had accused Job of denying that God punishes the wicked and that Job was merely trying to prove
that he was not suffering for sin. But what he just said
about the wicked proved that they were wrong. Job said,
"So then, who can make me out to be a liar? Who can
reduce my words to nothing?" (Job 24:25).

Job agreed with his friends: God calls the wicked to account for the evil they do. Previously, when Bildad had spoken about God's just treatment of the wicked (Job 8:11-22), Job agreed: "Of course I know that this is true" (Job 9:2). Later, after Zophar had made the same point, Job said, "But I understand these things as well as you. I do not fall short of you. Who doesn't know all these things?" (Job 12:3). Job agreed with his friends that in the end, God was just. What Job did not agree with was that they were applying this fact to him and to everyone who suffered. Job understood God's justice as well as they did. (24:25) But Job's question lingered: Why is God making me suffer?

Job 25 Bildad's third speech

Bildad responded with a short speech, after which the friends fell silent. They all considered Job's claim of innocence to be self-righteous foolishness. Bildad briefly repeated what he and the other two had said about God's power. He then pointed his finger at Job and contrasted God and sinful mortals. Since God does not find his own creation to be upright, "how much less a man, who is a maggot, and a son of man, who is a worm?" (Job 25:6). (25:1-6)

Job 26 Job's response to Bildad

Job responded with several verses of well-deserved sarcasm: "How marvelously you have helped the helpless!" (Job 26:2). "Who helped you proclaim these words? Whose breath came out of your mouth?" (Job 26:4). Bildad, he asked, whose breath (the Hebrew word can

185

also be translated "spirit") came out of your mouth? It certainly wasn't the breath of God!

Bildad claimed that Job didn't understand the almighty nature of God—that Job had reduced God to someone with whom a person could argue and criticize for acting unjustly. But Job had done nothing of the sort. He made it clear that he agreed with his friends about the power of God. After his description of the various aspects of God's power, he added a forceful exclamation point:

> But all these are just the fringe of his ways!
> How faint a whisper we hear of him!
> Who understands his power, which is displayed in
> the thunder? (Job 26:14) (26:1-14)

Special Topic: Job's Gospel Hope

Throughout his struggle with his friends' sinful ideas about God, he continued to confess God's forgiving love. When he struggled to decide which God to follow—God, who seemed to be unjust, or God, whose love he treasured, he always chose the latter. This is the essence of what James called Job's "steadfastness" (ESV), "perseverance" (NIV), "endurance" (NAS), and "patience" (KJV).

Job's statements of hope in God appear out of the blue. They are always bracketed by his struggle against suffering and the false wisdom of his friends. In this special topic we will look at Job's words of hope and include the context in which they were spoken.

Job 6:8-13 *"I have not denied the words of the Holy One."*

In chapter 3 Job had said he wished he were dead. In these verses from chapter 6, he wished for the same but for a different reason. He asked God to go all the way and kill him:

> If only my request would be granted.
> If only God would grant me what I hope for:
> that God would decide to crush me,
> that he would unleash his hand and cut me off.
> (Job 6:8,9)

And then he gave the reason for this request:

> For then I would still have this comfort:
> Even as I writhe in relentless pain,
> I have not denied the words of the Holy One.
> (Job 6:10)

Job's primary concern was not his suffering. Rather, it was to avoid rejecting what God had revealed to him: that God was gracious to him and had forgiven him. God's grace meant everything to Job. Holding on to the grace of God was more important than staying alive.

But immediately after he said this, Job started to complain again. His strength was gone. There was nothing ahead but a painful deathwatch. He didn't think he was strong enough to make it to the end with his faith intact.

> What strength do I have to wait hopefully?
> What end awaits me that would make me want to prolong my life?
> Is my strength like stone,
> or is my flesh bronze?
> Certainly I have no power to help myself,

since the hope that I can recover has been driven far
away from me. (Job 6:11-13)

Job 9:14-21 *"I can only plead to my judge for grace."*

Job knew he was innocent. But he was suffering. So he
wanted to talk with God and find out what he had done
to deserve this. That's what he meant when he said: "I
want to match words with him" (Job 9:14).

But as soon as the request came out of his mouth, he
realized how foolish it was. Even if Job was right and
did not deserve to be afflicted (which is what God
himself said in Job 2:3), it was still a frightening thing
to argue with God. And considering the fact that he *was*
right and was still being afflicted by God, he concluded
that God would not give him a straight answer. In fact,
he feared that God would make things worse. He said:

> But even if I am in the right, I cannot answer him.
> I can only plead to my judge for grace.
> If I called and he responded to me,
> I do not believe that he would listen to my voice.
> With a violent storm he would crush me,
> and he would inflict many wounds on me *for no reason.*
> He would not allow me to catch my breath.
> Instead, he would fill me with bitter experiences.
> If it is a question of strength, he definitely is the strong
> one.
> If it is a question of jurisdiction, who can summon him?
> (Job 9:15-19)

You probably caught the example of Job's hope mixed in
with his pessimism. No matter how innocent Job might
be, no matter how wrong the friends were to accuse

him of committing special sins, when he was in God's presence he would only pray for mercy.

> Even if I am righteous, my mouth would still condemn me.
> If I am blameless, it would pronounce me crooked.
> Although I am blameless, I cannot evaluate myself.
> I reject my own life. (Job 9:20-21)

A sinner cannot stand proudly before God. God's mercy is the only thing that gives a person, even a blameless person like Job, the courage to stand in his presence. This was part of Job's perseverance..

Job 13:13-16 *"Even if he slays me, I will wait for him with hope."*

Job wanted his day in court, convinced that he could successfully defend his innocence. But Job knew the precarious nature of his request. How can a mortal defend himself before God? Such a challenge to God might mean death.

He said:

> Silence! Let me speak.
> I intend to speak up, no matter what happens.
> Why do I bite my flesh with my teeth?
> Why do I take my life in my hands? (Job 13:13,14)

A sinner who wants to stand in God's presence invites death. But a forgiven sinner who wants to approach God boldly expects mercy. That's what Job expected, but the power of his friend's work-righteous logic said otherwise. The friends said, "Watch out. Don't get too close. You are a sinner." Job, in faith, said "If I were a sinner, it would be stupid for me to approach him."

Yet his suffering seemed to prove that God was angry with him and might kill him. But in the face of that possibility, Job said, "Even if he slays me, I will wait for him with hope. No matter what, I will defend my ways to his face" (Job 13:15). Job added: "Even this may turn out for my salvation, for no godless person would dare to face him"(Job 13:16).

With those words Job pictured God ready to slay him, but then stopping to reconsider: "What sinner would be so stupid to approach me. But wait, he must really be innocent if he is willing to accept the possibility of death."

Job 14:11-20 *"I will wait until change comes about for me."*

> Waters evaporate from the sea.
> A river dries up and becomes dust.
> In the same way, a man lies down and does not rise again.
> Until the heavens pass away, he does not awaken,
> and he is not aroused from his sleep. (Job 14:11,12)

That describes death. There is nothing more.

But Job said that even death could not stop God's love for him. Job knew the finality to death, but he also knew the never-ending nature of God's love. God might even change the nature of death to give God more time to love him.

Job asked God to hide him in the grave until God decided that his anger against Job had lasted long enough. When that time came, God would long for Job's company once again. Job put it this way:

> Oh how I wish you would hide me in the grave,

that you would conceal me until your wrath has passed
by,
that you would set an appointed time for me,
and then you would remember me.
If a man dies, will he live again?
Through all the days of my warfare,
I will wait, until change comes about for me.
You will call, and I myself will answer.
Then you will long for the work of your hands.
(Job 14:13-15)

At the present time, God was apparently keeping track
of Job's sins. But Job was sure that a time would come
when God would no longer keep track of them:

Now you count my steps,
but then you will no longer keep track of my sin.
My rebellious deeds will be sealed up in a bag,
and you will plaster over my guilt. (Job 14:16,17)

But as happened so often, Job turned his eyes away
from God's promises and focused on his suffering. Once
again, he viewed his situation as hopeless:

But as a mountain crumbles and falls,
and as a rock is moved from its place,
as water wears away stones,
and floodwaters wash away soil from the land,
so you destroy a man's hope. (Job 14:18,19)

Job 16:16-22 "My advocate is on high."

Job could not reconcile his innocence with the suffering
God had sent into his life. God's anger seemed unrelenting:

My face is red from my weeping.

> There are dark circles under my eyes,
> even though there is no violence in my hands,
> and my prayer is pure. (Job 16:16,17):

Yet Job knew that God's justice is overshadowed by his mercy. Job continued by saying

> O earth, do not cover my blood.
> Let my cry never find a place to rest.
> Even now, my witness is in heaven.
> My advocate is on high.
> My intercessor is my friend.
> My eyes never stop weeping to God.
> My intercessor pleads with God for a man,
> as another human pleads for his friend. (Job 16:18-21)

Job knew that at that very moment he had a witness before God, testifying to Job's faith and to Job's works of service to God. He called this person an advocate, a defense lawyer, who was right then pleading to God to be merciful to Job. Indeed, the advocate was someone human like Job but able to come before God on a man's behalf.

Sadly, however, Job's sense of hopelessness returned. "A few more years will come. Then I will go the way of no return."(Job 16:22).

Job 17:1-3,6,7 *"Who else could guarantee this payment for me?"*

At the beginning of this chapter, Job was still expressing his hopelessness:

> My spirit is broken.
> My days are snuffed out.
> The tomb is waiting for me.

192

Surely mockery closes in on me.
My eyes must live with my enemies' bitter contempt.
(Job 17:1,2)

Nevertheless, the hope Job had spoken about in chapter 16 once again rose to the surface. Job saw himself standing before the Judge. He wanted to argue his case and be freed from his suffering and from God's anger. But he could have his day in court only if someone posted bond for him.

Job confessed that no human being was able do that. Only God was. So Job pleaded:

Please pay for me the deposit [the bond] that you require from me.
Indeed, who else could guarantee this payment for me?
(Job 17:3)

Once again, however, Job was overwhelmed by his suffering:

He has made me a laughingstock among the people.
They spit in my face.
My vision is blurry from grief.
I am just a shadow of myself. (Job 17:6,7)

Job 19:6-8,20-27 "My Redeemer lives."

In chapter 19, Job continued to complain about his suffering. In a rather lengthy section, he accused God of acting unjustly toward him. Job said to his friends:

You should know that God has denied me justice,
and he has trapped me in his net.
Listen to me!
I cry out, "Injustice," but I get no answer.
I call for help, but there is no justice.

He has blocked my way, so I cannot get by.
He has brought darkness on my paths. (Job 19:6-8)

Job then continued with a long list of the unfair things
God had done to him. He ended by lumping God and
his friends together. They were both pursuing him:

I am nothing but skin and bones.
I have escaped with the skin of my teeth.
Have mercy on me.
Have mercy on me, you friends of mine,
because the hand of God has struck me.
Why do you pursue me the way God does?
Will you never get enough of my flesh? (Job 19:20-22)

Job could not have accused God more strongly. But
out of the blue, Job's hope rose to its greatest height.
He wanted the world to know about his hope in God's
mercy:

Oh how I wish that my words were written down.
Oh how I wish that they were inscribed in bronze,
that they would be engraved in rock forever
with an iron tool and letters filled with lead.
(Job 19:23,24)

What words were those? Job boldly proclaimed:

As for me, I know that my Redeemer lives,
and that at the end of time he will stand over the dust.
Then, even after my skin has been destroyed,
nevertheless, in my own flesh I will see God.
I myself will see him.
My own eyes will see him, and not as a stranger.
My emotions are in turmoil within me. (Job 19:25-27)

"Redeemer" is the translation of "goel," someone who
gets a relative out of trouble. Job knew that he had a
Redeemer and that his Redeemer was alive. Job's Goel
would remain standing when all else was destroyed, and
Job knew that he would see him with his own eyes.

In light of this, in the last two verses of this chapter, Job
warned his friends: "Do you think the problem is with
me, that I am getting what I deserve? If so, then judge
your own selves before it's too late. Otherwise, without
a Redeemer, you will get what you deserve at the final
judgment." He said to them:

> If you say, "What can we do to pursue him?"
> and "He is the root of his own problems,"
> then you should fear the edge of the sword for yourselves!
> For wrath brings the punishment of the sword,
> so that you will know that there is judgment.
> (Job 19:28,29)

Job 23:2-17 Job's perseverance amid struggles

Job's great testimony of faith in chapter 19 did not bring
his struggle to an end. We conclude this special topic
with a set of verses that illustrate how confidence and
doubt continued to be intermingled in Job's thoughts.

Job struggled:

> Even today my complaint is bitter.
> His hand weighs heavily on me despite my groaning.
> I wish I knew where I could find him,
> so that I could come to his place for judgment.
> Then I would lay out my case before him,
> and I would fill my mouth with arguments. (Job 23:2-4)

195

But he persevered:

> I would know what words he would use to respond to
> me,
> and I would consider what he would say to me.
> Would he use his great power to press charges against
> me?
> No, he will certainly give me a hearing. There, an upright
> man could argue with him,
> and I would be delivered from my judge forever.
> (Job 23:5-7)

Job struggled:

> But if I walk to the east, he is not there.
> If I go back to the west, I find no sign of him.
> When he is at work in the north, I do not detect him.
> When he turns to the south, I do not see him.
> (Job 23:8,9)

But he persevered:

> But I am sure he knows the way I take.
> When he has tested me, I will come out like gold.
> My feet have followed his footsteps closely.
> I have kept to his way, and I have not turned aside.
> I have not departed from the command from his lips.
> I have treasured the sayings from his mouth in my heart.
> (Job 23:10-12)

Job struggled:

> He stands alone.
> Who can make him change?
> Whatever his soul desires, he will do.
> He carries out his decrees against me,
> and he has so many of them!

> That is why I am in a panic in his presence.
> When I think about this, I dread him.
> God has made me lose heart.
> The Almighty has terrified me. (Job 23:13-16)

But again, he persevered:

> Nevertheless, I am not silenced by the darkness,
> by the dark cloud that covers my face. (Job 23:17)

Only forgiven sinners can be sure that God will not press charges against them. And although Job thought that God was not listening to him, he knew he was. Job persevered in that knowledge. Although God would rebuke Job for questioning his justice, at the end of the book God could still call Job "my servant" (Job 42:7,8).

Chapter 9

Job's Final Words—Job 27–31

Getting Into the Book

Reading—Chapters 27–31

Job 27 *Job begins his final speech*

Verses 1-6

> God is not just to send suffering and bitterness into my life. But as long as I live, I will never admit to your analysis of my sufferings. I will never let you give me a guilty conscience over sins I have not committed. I will never deny that I am blameless and upright. I will never deny my righteous service to God.

Verses 7-10

> Those who oppose my faith and my life—which I have lived in the fear of the Lord—will end up like the wicked. They have no delight in the Lord, and he will not listen to their prayers.

Verses 11-23

> Let me explain what God will do to the wicked—
> I'm referring to you, my friends. Sword, hunger, and
> plague will spoil their lives. They will die, and even
> their widows will not mourn for them. Their posses-
> sions and clothing will be given to the poor. Their
> houses will be crushed like a moth's cocoon. They
> will come to ruin suddenly. The destructive forces of
> nature will sweep over them. They will try to escape,
> but won't be able to.

Job 28 *Job tells his friends where true wisdom can be found*

Verses 1-11

> With much ingenuity and toil, people can find pre-
> cious metals hidden in the earth. Miners dig deep,
> swinging from ropes in the shafts they have dug.
> They know how to find where silver and gold are
> plenteous.
>
> The birds and animals don't know how they do this.
> But they dig tunnels deep in the earth. They dam up
> rivers to find the gold hidden on the river bottoms.

Verses 12-19

> But wisdom is a rare commodity that no human
> being can find on their own. It can't be found in
> the ocean. It can't be bought from traders, no mat-
> ter how large a payment the purchaser might offer.
> Even a payment of pure gold and precious jewels is
> not enough.

Verses 20-22

On earth, people cannot find it. In the air, the birds have not seen it. Nor does the underworld know where to find it, even though it has heard that such a thing exists.

Verses 23-28

God alone understands everything about the world. And as far as human beings are concerned, this is wisdom. God says to us, "Listen carefully. The fear of the Lord—that is wisdom, and to turn away from evil is understanding" (Job 29:28).

Job 29 *Job describes what his life has been like*

Verses 1-25

How I yearn for the days when God was still with me! He led me by his light and gave me his friendly counsel. He showered blessings on me and my household. When I went to the city gate to serve on the town council, young men stepped aside, and the elders stood as I passed by. They remained quiet until I gave my advice.

Everyone blessed me and took my advice. God gave me wisdom, resources, and a gracious spirit so that I could help the needy. I acted in righteousness and justice. I anticipated my life ending like that. People listened to me as I spoke gentle words to them. They waited for me like they wait for a refreshing rain shower. They were never downcast when I was near. I led them, and I comforted them.

Job 30 *Job describes what his life is like now*

Verses 1–15

There was a time when I wouldn't have hired certain men to watch my sheep. They were a wretched brood, shunned by everyone. But now their sons mock and scorn me. They keep their distance. They spit in my face.

God has withdrawn his protecting hand from me. Now there is nothing to keep these men from attacking me. They trip me up, block my escape, take advantage of my weakness, and loot my property. I have no prestige, no security, and I live in terror.

Verses 16–31

Night and day my body and soul are racked with pain. God tears at my clothing, choking my neck. He has cast me into the mud, made me dust and ashes, and pays no attention to my cry for help. I am blown away by the wind, tossed by the storms, and near death. I am destroyed. O God, why won't you help me?

I helped others who were suffering, but now I am suffering and no one helps me, not even God. Day after day God afflicts me. All I can do is mourn and wail in my distress. I am an outcast. My skin blackens and falls off. I have no joy in life.

Job 31 *Job resolves to continue in the fear of the Lord*

Verses 1–40

Yet I will maintain my integrity.

From my youth I have kept my conscience pure. I did not give in to lust, for that would have led to my ruin.

Ruin comes to the wicked, but since God sees everything I do, he knows me to be blameless.

If I have taken what is not mine, then may my possessions become the property of others.

If I have committed adultery, then let someone commit adultery with my wife, and may I come to ruin.

If I have mistreated my servants, how could I excuse myself to God? After all, we are both his creations.

Did I hoard my food and refuse to share it with the poor, the widow, and the fatherless? No. From my youth I helped the needy, and they blessed me for it.

Did I take advantage of an orphan in a court of law? If so, let God punish me for it.

Did I rely on my riches? Did I worship the sun and the moon? If I had, I would be guilty of denying the Lord.

Have I ever cursed my neighbor or refused to help someone who needed food or shelter?

Did I ever conceal my sin for fear of what people might do to me?

Oh, that God would listen to me and tell me how I have sinned. Let him give me a written description of my life. If he did, I would wear it like a crown on my head to show everyone that I am innocent of all charges. But if I have sinned and not lived in the fear of the Lord, I will gladly stand condemned and accept my punishment.

One more thing. If I've ever robbed my neighbor's produce or killed him to get his field, then may those fields produce thorns and stinkweeds.

The words of Job are concluded. There was nothing more he could say.

Looking at Job

Job 27 Job begins his final speech

At this point, Job began his bottom-line statement—the position from which he refused to budge. It will continue through chapter 31.

Job began, "As God lives, he has deprived me of justice. The Almighty has made my life bitter" (Job 27:2). Job was right about God making his life bitter. Job sinned, however, by claiming that God was unjust in doing so. This is the sin alluded to by the writer of Job when Job first spoke about his losses and later when he rebuked his wife. Each time the writer added that Job said nothing wrong: "In all this, Job did not sin or blame God" and "In all this, Job did not sin in what he said" (Job 1:22; 2:10).

But when his friends brought up the topic of God's justice, which they did in every one of their speeches, Job felt justified to ask God how he could justly send suffering into the life of an innocent man. When he did that, Job sinned *in what he said*. (27:1,2)

Job's friends never told Job to curse God as his wife had done, but they tried to protect God's justice by finding in Job the reason for why God was afflicting him. Job, however, resolved to remain faithful to God. He would never let thoughts of God's injustice force him to give up his wisdom and adopt the wisdom of his friends. He said, "May I be cursed if I ever admit you are right. Until I die, I will never deny my integrity" (Job 27:5). He would never admit that he was wicked, because he wasn't. He said adamantly, "I have held tight to my righteousness, and I will not let it go" (Job 27:6). This was not a statement of proud work-righteousness but the statement of a humble servant of God pointing to what God had done in his heart. And to deny his past service to God was to deny God's promise of a Savior, who was the sole reason for why he served God. (27:3-6)

In chapter 24, Job agreed with his friends that God judges the wicked. In chapter 26, Job agreed with his friends that God has power to do whatever he wants. In the rest of the present chapter, however, Job turned the tables and applied these truths to his friends. He said to them, "May my enemy be like the wicked. May the one who rises up against me be like the unjust" (Job 27:7). The friends had been telling Job that God was angry with him. Here Job told his friends that God was angry with them. Job was right. After it was all over, God himself said to Eliphaz: "My anger burns against you and your two friends, because none of you have spoken correctly about me, as my servant Job did" (Job 42:7). (27:7)

Job then described to his friends what God does to wicked people—and he was referring to his friends. His words paralleled his friends' previous description of what they thought God would do to him. For example, Job says,

> He goes to bed as a rich man,
> but his wealth does not remain.
> He opens his eyes, and it is all gone.
> Terrors sweep over him like floodwaters.
> At night, a strong wind carries him away. (Job 27:19,20)
> (27:8-23)

Job 28 *Job tells where true wisdom can be found*

The book of Job is a struggle to speak wisely about why God made Job suffer. Job's friends claimed that their wisdom came from people who lived long ago, in ancient times. As we have seen, their wisdom was simple. The righteous are blessed, and the wicked are cursed.

Job's wisdom was different. His wisdom began and ended with his shunning evil out of honor, respect, and love for God. He focused on God's blessings. He loved God because he knew God's promise of a Savior from sin. He lived in the joy that he could offer God sacrifices for the sins of his children and know that God would accept them.

If Job rejected his friends' wisdom, then he should be able to tell them where true wisdom can be found. Yet all he could say was, "But wisdom—where can it be found? Where is the place for understanding?" (Job 28:12).

There are certain things that human beings are good at finding. People dig for gold and with much effort they dig it out. The friends thought that finding wisdom was like finding gold. It can be found by careful study. The friends had found it in the words of their forefathers. (28:1-11)

But were they right? Job answered: "Mankind does not know where it is kept. It is not found in the land of the living" (Job 28:13). The ocean doesn't know where it is. It is worth far more than the finest jewelry and the rarest stones. "It cannot be purchased even with pure gold" (Job 28:19).

Job repeated, "But what about wisdom—where does it come from?" (Job 28:20). Even Destruction and Death—the place that has firsthand knowledge of the judgment God brings on the wicked—must admit, "With our ears we have heard only a rumor about it" (Job 28:22). (28:12-22)

Only God knows where to find wisdom: "God understands the way to it, and he alone knows its place" (Job 28:23). What no human being can understand, God understands clearly: "He saw wisdom and appraised its value. He established it and also explored it" (Job 28:27). (28:23-27)

Job knew that his friends had *not* found true wisdom. God does not share details about how his wisdom works in how he administers justice in any given situation. In view of that, Job lived wisely following God's description of true wisdom: "Then [God] said to mankind: Listen carefully. The fear of the Lord—that is wisdom, and to turn away from evil is understanding" (Job 28:28).

Can the kind of wisdom the friends were searching for, and which they thought they had discovered, actually be found? Job said, no. When you observe what actually happens in the lives of the wicked and the righteous, you will be forced to admit that you cannot figure out a pattern that God has bound himself to follow. True wisdom is not to explore the hidden things of God—the "why" of God's actions in the world. Rather, it is to live one's life on the basis of what he has revealed to us. Rest in his mercy and forgiveness. Praise him for that and praise him for what he brings into your life—when he gives and when he takes away, when he gives good things as well as when he gives bad things. In all things, fear the Lord and give up evil. (28:28)

***Job 29** Job describes what his life had been like*

Job had followed that course of action: He feared the Lord and shunned evil. We heard this three times in the first two chapters. Everything went well for him, but then suddenly everything went badly for him. In chapter 30, Job described what his life used to be like. In chapter 31, he will describe how his life had changed ever since God made him suffer.

Job's "then and now" contrast was a statement of fact. But it also shows that what he said to his wife—that God has the right to give bad things as well as good things—was being influenced by his friends' wisdom.

Consider how he began: "Oh how I wish I could be as I used to be in the months gone by, in the days when God used to watch over me" (Job 29:2). We certainly don't begrudge Job the right to yearn for the return of those wonderful days. But when Job said: ". . . in the days when God *used to* watch over me, . . . when the Almighty *was still* with me" (Job 29:2,5), we realize that Job considered the change in his life to be a change in God. God *used to* be with him. It was a time when God was *still* watching over him and directing his steps. But that time was over. Back then Job anticipated that nothing would change for him: "So I thought: 'I will pass away in my own nest, after multiplying my days like grains of sand'" (Job 29:18). But no more. (29:1-5)

The change that took place in Job's life was heart wrenching. Job's description is easily understood, so we will not comment on the specifics. But one thing is striking: Notice that Job did not primarily find joy in his possessions, position, and wisdom. Rather, he refers to the joy he brought into the lives of the people around him as he used his blessings in the fear of the Lord. That's what he missed the most. (29:6-25)

Job 30 Job describes what his life is like now

Job then described his life after his suffering began. Again, he described its effect on the people around him—how their former respect for him had turned into scorn. Young people whose fathers Job would never have hired now mocked him. (30:1-10)

God had done this to him: "God has unhooked my bowstring, and he has afflicted me, so they [the young men referred to above] throw off all restraint in my presence" (Job 30:11). God was cruel toward him and unresponsive to his plea for help. Job complained:

> God tugs violently at my clothing.
> He chokes me like the collar of my robe.
> He has thrown me into the mud,
> and I have become like dust and ashes.
> I cry to you for help, but you do not answer me.
> Whenever I stand up, you pay no attention to me.

> You have become cruel to me.
> With a strong hand you assault me. (Job 30:18-21)
> (30:11-23)

Job always came to the aid of those who sought his help. But now he was the one crying for help, but no one helped him: "But when I waited for good, evil came. When I hoped for light, darkness came" (Job 30:26). He ended on a note of sadness: "My lyre plays only sad songs. My flute accompanies only the sound of weeping" (Job 30:31). (30:24-31)

Job 31 Job resolves to continue in the fear of the Lord

Job agreed with his friends. God is just. He punishes the wicked and rewards the righteous. But as we have seen, Job did not agree with them about how God carries out his justice. Nor did he agree that blessings and sufferings can serve to identify who is righteous and who is wicked. He was confident that "if God weighs me on an honest scale, he will know my integrity" (Job 31:6).

Again, we note that Job was right. At the beginning of the book, God affirmed Job's righteousness. And later God boasted to Satan that Job was maintaining his integrity even after the loss of his possessions and family. But here Job implied that God was no longer using an honest scale to weigh Job's life against God's definition of righteousness. (31:1-6)

To prove that he had, in fact, lived righteously, Job made a list of everything he had done in the fear of the Lord, calling down a curse on himself if he was lying. For example, he began:

> I have made a covenant with my eyes.

How then could I stare at a virgin with desire?
If I did, what reward would I receive from God above?
What inheritance from the Almighty on high?
Is not ruin the reward for the wicked,
and misfortune the reward for evildoers? (Job 31:1-3)

He was willing to have God examine every area of his life. He was confident that God would find him innocent. He would accept God's judgment if he had

... covered up my sin like Adam,
and ... hidden my guilt in my heart,
because I was frightened of the crowd,
and the contempt of the clans filled me with terror.
(Job 31:33,34)

But he had not covered up sin. He had done nothing shameful to spoil his relationship with his neighbors and hinder his service to them. (31:7-34)

Job yearned for someone to listen to him. "I am testifying to my innocence," he said. He wanted God to tell him what he was doing wrong, "Let me see the written indictment from my accuser" (Job 31:35).

Job was confident that God's verdict on his life would be "not guilty." He knew he was not guilty by virtue of God's forgiveness. But for that reason, he had done nothing other than live a "blameless and upright life" as the writer of Job and God himself had said three times in the first two chapters. Therefore, he would wear God's verdict like "a crown" (Job 31:36). And if God would ever give him a hearing, Job would "account to him for every single step" and approach God "like the chief of a tribe" (Job 31:37). (31:35-37)

Job ended with one other example of his righteousness. If he had robbed anyone of their land or harvested it without paying for its crops, then may God cover that parcel with weeds.

At this point the writer added, "The words of Job are concluded" (Job 31:40). Job had no more to say. He would never admit to a hidden sin for which he had not repented. He would never try to get rid of his suffering by trying to earn God's favor. As one person said, he would never turn his "done" religion into a "do" religion. Job was wrong to call God unjust, but he would never surrender the upright life he had lived out of love for God's mercy. (31:38-40)

Special Topic: Can Christians Appeal to Their Own Righteousness Without Being Work-righteous?

Throughout the book of Job, Job asserted that he lived a righteous life and that he was innocent of all the sins his friends claimed he had committed. At the end of his final speech, he concluded by describing the moral life he had lived. He also suggested a punishment he would readily accept if he was lying.

It sometimes sounds as if Job was work-righteous—that his innocent life had made him worthy of God's blessings. Some Christians are uncomfortable with Job's claim to innocence and that he saw no reason why God should be afflicting him.

We know that work-righteousness is always a danger. Jesus had to confront it. So did Paul. Paul wrote: "I do not set aside the grace of God, for if righteousness could be gained through the law, Christ died for nothing!" (Galatians 2:21).

Works play no role in a Christian's hope of heaven. Our good lives cannot make us worthy of God's promises. Old Testament believers knew this. God declared Abraham righteous because Abraham believed that God would give him an heir from whom the Savior would come:

> And Abram said, "Behold, you have given me no offspring, and a member of my household will be my heir." And behold, the word of the Lord came to him: "This man shall not be your heir; your very own son shall be your heir." And he brought him outside and said, "Look toward heaven, and number the stars, if you are able to number them." Then he said to him, "So shall your offspring be." And he believed the Lord, and he counted it to him as righteousness. (Genesis 15:3-6)

Job based his hope in his Redeemer, the advocate and witness he had before God in heaven. If Job had believed that his righteous life earned him the right to have a Redeemer, he never would have offered sacrifices for his children, asked God to pay the bond in God's court, or rejoiced that his sins would be sealed up and painted over. If he was work-righteous, he would never have wondered if his suffering was a sign that God had stopped forgiving him. And he would have accepted his friends' advice to get God to lift his suffering by living a more moral life. Job was not work-righteous.

But if not, why did Job so often appeal to his righteous life? What place did that have in the conversation with his friends or in his prayers to God? To answer that, it would be worthwhile to look at some of the many places in Scripture that link our assurance of God's blessings with the good works we do. The passages will be listed in a somewhat random order. Not all of them fit Job's situation exactly. But the list will help us put Job's claim of innocence in the proper light.

John 15:9,10

> "As the Father has loved me, so have I loved you. Abide in my love. If you keep my commandments, you will abide in my love, just as I have kept my Father's commandments and abide in his love."

Jesus loved his heavenly Father. Jesus' whole life reflected what he said in the Garden of Gethsemane: "Not as I will, but as you will" (Matthew 26:39). Accordingly, Jesus willingly gave himself into death for the world's sins because his Father wanted him to. Because of this, he remained in his Father's love. God testified to this when he said to the disciples on the Mount of Transfiguration: "This is my beloved Son, with whom I am well pleased; listen to him" (Matthew 17:5).

We are God's children, whom he loves. But to rebel against his will means that we reject his love and no longer want to be in his family. But like Jesus, when we follow his will, we remain in his love.

Galatians 5:6

Paul said much the same thing:

For in Christ Jesus neither circumcision nor uncircumcision counts for anything, but only faith working through love.

In the first part of the verse, Paul said we are saved through faith in Christ alone. In the second part he said that faith is always at work, producing fruits.

James 2:26

James said the same:

As the body without the spirit is dead, so faith without deeds is dead. (NIV84)

Romans 4:1-3,13; James 2:20-24; Genesis 22:15-18

Note the following set of passages about Abraham. The first is about Abraham's faith in God's promise. The second two are about Abraham's service to God, inspired by his faith in that promise.

Abraham was God's child through faith in God's promises alone. Paul made that point in Romans 4. He wrote:

What then shall we say that Abraham, our forefather, discovered in this matter? If, in fact, Abraham was justified by works, he had something to boast about—but not before God. What does the Scripture say? "Abraham believed God, and it was credited to him as righteousness." It was not through law that Abraham and his offspring received the promise that he would be heir of the world, but through the righteousness that comes by faith. (Romans 4:1-3,13 NIV84)

James, on the other hand, was speaking to people who had forgotten what Paul said in Ephesians 2:10: "For we are his workmanship, created in Christ Jesus for good works, which God prepared beforehand, that we should walk in them." So James focused on the fruits that Abraham's faith produced. He wrote:

> Do you want to be shown, you foolish person, that faith apart from works is useless? Was not Abraham our father justified by works when he offered up his son Isaac on the altar? You see that faith was active along with his works, and faith was completed by his works; and the Scripture was fulfilled that says, "Abraham believed God, and it was counted to him as righteousness"—and he was called a friend of God. You see that a person is justified by works and not by faith alone. (James 2:20-24)

God himself spoke the same way. In the Old Testament account James was referring to, Abraham was about ready to sacrifice his son as God had commanded him. But God told him to stop. And then God provided the sacrifice he required. Here is how the account ended:

> And the angel of the LORD called to Abraham a second time from heaven and said, "By myself I have sworn, declares the LORD, because you have done this and have not withheld your son, your only son, I will surely bless you, and I will surely multiply your offspring as the stars of heaven and as the sand that is on the seashore. And your offspring shall possess the gate of his enemies, and in your offspring shall all the nations of the earth be blessed, because you have obeyed my voice." (Genesis 22:15-18)

When God spoke to Abraham immediately after Abraham had followed a most difficult command, God naturally gave Abraham's faith-produced act as the reason why Abraham would receive his promises.

Anyone can turn this statement into work-righteousness. But it is simply Scripture's way of saying that faith is always living and active, and it shows itself by deeds of love for God.

Put Abraham in Job's place. If someone had said to Abraham, "You have no faith in God. You don't honor and respect him!" Abraham might have answered, "How can you say that? God told me to sacrifice my son, and I would have done it if he hadn't stopped me." In a nutshell, that's what Job was saying every time his friends accused him of acting wickedly against God. He was asking them, "How can you say that? Just look at my life!"

Matthew 25:20,21

Jesus often substituted works for faith when he spoke about believers. In the parable of the talents, when the master returned, he said to the faithful servant:

> "And he who had received the five talents came forward, bringing five talents more, saying, 'Master, you delivered to me five talents; here, I have made five talents more.' His master said to him, 'Well done, good and faithful servant. You have been faithful over a little; I will set you over much. Enter into the joy of your master.'"
> (Matthew 25:20,21)

The good manager loved his master. He knew he would someday share in the joy of his master's kingdom. So he continued to serve his master even though the master was absent. When the master returned, he pointed to the servant's faithful labor and rewarded him for it.

If we had been that servant and heard the master say to us, "Well done," we would never have replied, "But I am a sinner. I have not done well. I am saved by grace, through faith in what Jesus did for me." That statement is true, of course. But that's not what we will say. We wiyl humblt accept his praise because we know why we acted as we did.

Matthew 25:31-46

Immediately following the parable of the tenants is Jesus' description of the last day in the parable of the sheep and the goats. On that day, Jesus will point to the works done by the believers and the works unbelievers refused to do. The believers bore witness to their faith by caring for Jesus' brothers and sisters in their suffering and need. The unbelievers had no awareness that some people really were children of God and even despised those who claimed to be. For that reason, they did nothing to help them.

Jesus will use these criteria for whom he invites into Heaven and whom he consigns to Hell. Fear of work-righteousness should never lead us to downplay the fruits of our faith.

We dare never say that our good works are like filthy rags, which is how some interpret Isaiah 64:5-7:

> You come to the help of those who gladly do right, who remember your ways. But when we continued to sin against them, you were angry. How then can we be saved? All of us have become like one who is unclean, and all our righteous acts are like filthy rags; we all shrivel up like a leaf, and like the wind our sins sweep us away.

No one calls on your name or strives to lay hold of you;
for you have hidden your face from us and made us waste
away because of our sins. (NIV84)

In these verses, Isaiah was bemoaning the change in
Israel. They had turned from people who gladly did
what was right into people who were unclean. The
Israelites still offered sacrifices and kept God's other-
laws. But these "righteous" works, done from mere habit
or with work-righteous intent, had become unclean to
God, just as the ones who did them were unclean.

Psalm 7:3-10

Job's three friends charged Job with sin to justify their
false understanding of why God was afflicting him. In a
similar way, King David's enemies justified their attacks
on him with the claim that he was wicked. One time
David prayed: "Hear a just cause, O LORD; attend to
my cry! Give ear to my prayer from lips free of deceit!"
(Psalm 17:1).

In Psalm 7 David defended himself against the false
charges of his enemies just like Job defended himself
against the false charges of his friends. Notice the similarity of David's words to what Job said in Job 31.

David prayed:

O LORD my God, if I have done this
and there is guilt on my hands—
if I have done evil to him who is at peace with me
or without cause have robbed my foe—
then let my enemy pursue and overtake me;
let him trample my life to the ground
and make me sleep in the dust.

Arise, O LORD, in your anger;
rise up against the rage of my enemies.
Awake, my God; decree justice.
Let the assembled peoples gather around you.
Rule over them from on high;
let the LORD judge the peoples.
Judge me, O LORD, according to my righteousness,
according to my integrity, O Most High.
O righteous God, who searches minds and hearts,
bring to an end the violence of the wicked
and make the righteous secure.
My shield is God Most High,
who saves the upright in heart. (Psalm 7:3-10 NIV84)

David was not saying he was sinless any more than Job
was. They were both defending themselves against the
false charges of their enemies by pointing out that they
had served God.

Both David and Job trusted in God unfailing mercy,
which was why they could always be confident of God's
love. David ended Psalm 7 like this: "I will give thanks
to the LORD because of his righteousness and will sing
praise to the name of the LORD Most High" (Psalm 7:17
NIV84).

Romans 2:6-11

Here Paul is describing two ways people can live and
what will happend when they die.

[God] will render to each one according to his
works: to those who by patience in well-doing seek
for glory and honor and immortality, he will give
eternal life; but for those who are self-seeking and

do not obey the truth, but obey unrighteousness, there will be wrath and fury. There will be tribulation and distress for every human being who does evil, the Jew first and also the Greek, but glory and honor and peace for everyone who does good, the Jew first and also the Greek. For God shows no partiality.

Paul is saying no more than what Jesus said in the parable of the sheep and the goats in Matthew 25. This is how Paul lived his own life: "One thing I do: forgetting what lies behind and straining forward to what lies ahead, I press on toward the goal for the prize of the upward call of God in Christ Jesus" (Philippians 3:13-14). We fault neither Paul nor Job for pointing out their patient struggle to hold on to God's grace and serve him.

1 John 4:16-21

Consider these verses from John's first letter:

And so we know and rely on the love God has for us. God is love. Whoever lives in love lives in God, and God in him. In this way, love is made complete among us so that we will have confidence on the day of judgment, because in this world we are like him. There is no fear in love. But perfect love drives out fear, because fear has to do with punishment. The one who fears is not made perfect in love. We love because he first loved us. If anyone says, "I love God," yet hates his brother, he is a liar. For anyone who does not love his brother, whom he has seen, cannot love God, whom he has not seen. And he has given us this command: Whoever loves God must also love his brother. (1 John 4:16-21 NIV84)

God's love for us in Christ is perfect and complete from the moment we come to faith. However, there is another love—our love for God and our neighbor—which becomes more and more perfect as we live in Christ's love for us.

Here is how one well-known Lutheran commentator, George Stoeckhardt, interpreted this passage and the meaning of "love" in the phrase "love is made complete among us":

> This is said of the love that is with us, that dwells in us. It is our love, which has its origin in God. This love has reached its end and purpose when it enables us to face Judgment Day with confidence. By this everyone can test himself whether he really possesses this love, as he considers in what frame of mind he approaches Judgment Day. Whoever has this God-born love is not frightened at the thought of Judgment Day. He approaches this Day with fearless confidence. He enters the presence of the great Judge unafraid.
>
> ... We must remember that the Apostle at this place does not say how Christians, terrified about their sins, should meet the thought of Judgment Day. Only by faith in Christ, which apprehends the merits of Christ, can one stand before the Judge. That is here presupposed. From such faith necessarily flows love. That faith in Christ quiets our heart against sin, we have read earlier in this epistle. Yet what the Apostle writes here is meant to test our faith. Are we terrified by the thought of Judgment! We ought not be. Our love is an evidence of faith.[6]

---

[6] George Stoeckhart, *Lectures on the Three Letters of John*, tr. Hugo W. Degner. Atkin, Minnesota: Hope Press, 1963), pp. 107-109. George Stoeckhart taught Bible interpretation at Concordia

Christ's forgiveness is the sinners' only source of hope. But in the face of accusations that we are godless and cannot stand in the judgment—even when those accusations come from our own consciences—our life of service plays a role. If we become afraid of Judgment Day, we simply look at the love we show to God and our brothers and sisters. We see that we are acting toward others like God acts toward us. This shows that we are like him, and because we are like him, we have no fear of meeting hin on Judgment Day. This is an encouragement for us to grow in love.

Our struggle against work-righteousness is never-ending. But the answer is not to downplay the good works we do, or to necessarily make it wrong to appeal to those good works when we are affirming the genuineness of our faith.

This is what Job was doing. Although his frustration with his friends and his feeling that God was treating him unjustly may at times have colored his words, he was not boasting. He was defending the truth of what God himself had said about him in chapter 1, and he was protecting what God had done and was still doing in him. He was saying nothing other than what Paul told the Corinthians: "His grace toward me was not in vain. On the contrary, I worked harder than any of them, though it was not I, but the grace of God that is with me."(1 Corinthians 15:10).

⟿

Seminary, St. Louis, from 1878 to 1913. He was the Missouri Synod's first great exegete, working closely with C. F. W. Walther..

Chapter 10

Elihu Counseled Job—Job 32–37

Getting Into the Book

Reading—Chapters 32–37

Job 32 *Verses 1-14*

A fourth friend, Elihu, began to speak. He said

I am younger than you. So I waited until you were finished before I spoke. But I must speak because I am angry. I am angry with Job because he considers himself more just than God. And I am angry with you "friends" because you've condemned Job but have not produced any reason for why you are condemning him.

You are old. But old people aren't automatically wise. Wisdom comes from God. I listened carefully as you spoke and have thought about it. None of you knows why Job is acting wrongly. And don't claim that since Job doesn't accept your words it's up to God to convince Job that you are right.

Job has not been arguing with me, and I have a new way of explaining why he is suffering.

Verses 5-22

Now that you three can find nothing more to say, I will speak. Indeed, I must speak. I have much to say, and if I remain silent, I will burst. So I will speak and find relief.

I will not win Job over with flattery. I will say exactly what I think. In fact, I couldn't use flattery because I know it is hypocritical and a sin against God

Job 33 *Verses 1-4*

Job, listen to what I have to say. I am carefully putting my thoughts into words. You will find them clear and upright.

Verses 5-7

I am speaking on God's behalf. Yet I am a man just like you. So don't be afraid of what I have to say. Consider this a discussion. Refute me if you can.

Verses 8-13

You are not right in claiming to be innocent. I heard you say the following: "I am pure, without sinful rebellion. I am clean. I have no guilt." You claim that God has trumped up charges against you and treats you like his enemy, a criminal who needs to be watched.

I must object. It is not right to say such things. God is greater than you are. His ways are right.

Verses 14–22

> God may not be speaking to you as you expect him
> to. But he is, in fact, speaking to you. It might be
> through a dream in which he warns you to change
> your ways to keep you from dying in sin. It might be
> through suffering, even suffering so horrible that you
> seem to be close to death.

Verses 23–28

> There is, in fact, a mediator between you and God.
> This mediator is telling you the right thing to do.
> But most important, he is asking God to save you
> from death because he has given you a ransom.

> If you believe this, you will be filled with joy. You
> will pray to God, and you will find a friend in him.
> He will restore your righteousness. If you believe
> this, you will be filled with joy. You will pray to God,
> and you will find a friend in him. He will restore
> you. Then you will tell people that you are forgiven
> and did not get what your sins deserved. You will
> not die but live.

Verses 29–33

> Job, you are God's child. He is chastening you like a
> father chastens his child. He does this often to turn
> people from their sins and give them hope.

> Job, answer me: Am I wrong? Convince me that I
> am, and I will agree that you are innocent. Other-
> wise, keep listening for I have more wisdom to share.

Job 34 *Verses 1-15*

You wise men, let us carefully determine the truth and choose our words carefully.

Job says that he is innocent and that God has robbed him of justice.

In saying that God is unjust, Job is in error. Such thoughts put him in company with the wicked. What's more, since he thinks that he is innocent, his suffering has led him to conclude that serving God is worthless.

You wise men, listen to what I have to say. God does nothing wrong. He is perfectly just, always causing people's sins to catch up with them. God is in charge of the entire world, a position no one in the world had the power to bestow on him. His spirit resides in all people, and if God would withdraw it, everyone would die.

Verses 16-37

Job, listen to me. Since God governs all things, it is impossible that he hates justice. He labels wicked rulers for what they are. He creates people of high and low position, and he deals with them impartially.

All people die as God determines. God sees all things, and there is no place the wicked can hide. God does not need a lengthy investigation of the lives of rulers. He quickly deposes one and sets another in his place. He strikes them down because they did not follow his ways, but rather afflicted the poor.

If God might remain silent in the face of wickedness, he is still in charge and he keeps the wicked from ruling.

Job, God does not owe you anything. Even if you went so far as to confess your sins, ask God to point out any that you've missed, and then promise not to repeat them, even then God would be under no obligation to forgive you. Speak up, Job, and tell me what you know.

We all agree that Job does not understand what he is saying, and his words are wicked and rebellious. They show only contempt for God. I wish he were tested even more.

Job 35 Verses 1-9

Job, how can you say that your righteousness is greater than God's? How can you say it does no good to live an upright life?

You and your friends think that living righteously has a great effect on God. But look into the height of heaven. God is far above us. How does your righteous life affect him? Nor do the evil things you have done. In truth, your way of life affects only yourself and the people around you.

Verses 10-16

Wicked people cry out, but God does not answer them. That's because their prayers are offered in pride and insincerity. How much less does he answer impatient prayers such as yours—you who demand an audience with God.

You question the way God deals with sin. You speak without understanding.

Job 36 *Verses 1-14*

Job, I have more to say, so please listen. I understand God, and I will tell you about him.

God is great, but he does not despise us. True, he punishes the wicked, and he exalts the righteous. But in some cases, if he causes righteous people to suffer, he does it for a purpose. He is disciplining them, trying to make them give up sins they are committing. If they listen, they will be blessed. If not, they will be swept away and die. The wicked become angry when this happens. But they will die in their wickedness anyway.

Verses 15-21

God uses suffering to deliver us. That's what he is doing for you. He has hemmed you in for the purpose of giving you freedom. This suffering will lead to blessing. But by your words, you reject this, and your attitude puts you among the wicked.

Do not let anything lure you away from the purpose of your sufferings. Do not yearn for death. Use the time you have left to repent, which is what God wants you to do. But sadly, you seem to prefer sin.

Verses 22-33

I have more to say.

God has great wisdom. Who can instruct him? Who can criticize what he does?

How can we not praise him? Consider his creation. Everyone is amazed at it, even though they see it from a distance. No one can fully comprehend God or his eternal nature. He established the water cycle. He sends rain. He understands how the clouds work. He understands thunder and lightning. He knows what is on the bottom of the sea.

He can use all these things as tools for judgment, or he can use them to bless us. He is like a warrior, charging ahead with lightning and thunder. Why, even the animals sense the impending storm.

Job 37 *Verses 1-13*

Just look at what God can do! It makes me shudder.

The lightning flashes and his voice thunders. What amazing things his voice causes—things we cannot fully understand. He sends snow and unstoppable rainstorms. Although mankind makes plans, God is the one in complete control. When winter approaches, the wild animals look for dens. God brings the cold and makes the ice. The rain clouds swirl over the face of the earth, and he controls their every movement—whether to bring judgment or blessing.

Verses 14-20

Job, when you reflect on God's greatness, how can you presume to demand an audience with him? Do you understand how his creation works? How about the sun, which sometimes hides behind the clouds and sometimes shines in full force—so much so that you must work hard to escape its heat!

So how can you make a case against him? How can you demand an audience with him? You may as well ask that he swallow you up.

Verses 21–33

You cannot look into the sun in its full brilliance. Nor can you look directly at God's glory. You can only see him as he approaches out of the north in a storm.

Nevertheless, he is just and righteous. And he has regard for all who are wise.

Looking at Job

Job 32 Elihu introduces himself

Job's friends had no more to say. Job had stated his position. He would not accept his friends' explanation for why he was suffering.

Another person began to speak. The writer of the book identifies him as "Elihu son of Barakel, the Buzite, from the clan of Ram" (Job 32:2). He was a younger man, who had deferred to the other three because they were older than him.

Elihu was angry at both Job and his friends. He felt justified to feel that way. Job, in his discussion with his friends, had called God unjust. The friends said that Job was suffering because he refused to give up sin, but they had no proof that he had sinned. They could only speculate about what Job might have done. (32:1-5)

Elihu believed that he had the answer to why Job was suffering. But because he was younger than the three friends, he had not joined the conversation. After listening to them, he concluded that their wisdom was no wisdom at all. Wisdom, he said, does not necessarily come from one's elders. It comes from the Spirit of God. He would offer Job a different way of thinking about his suffering. (32:6-14) He would not speak insincerely but with brutal honesty. (32:15-22)

Job 33 *Elihu begins speaking to Job*

Elihu asked for Job's attention. He would speak on God's behalf, clearly and honestly. (33:1-4)

If he wished, Job should feel free to respond to what Elihu had to say and prove him wrong. Both he and Job were human beings made by the same Creator. Elihu said he would speak convincingly but that he was not trying to intimidate Job. (33:5-7)

As with everything Elihu said, the reader must determine how they will "hear" Elihu. Did he speak proudly, pompously, angrily, or coldly? Some hear him that way. Or did he speak with love and in a calm but firm voice? Others hear him like that. Did Elihu raise his voice to make his points? Perhaps he did.

In any case, if we accept what Elihu said about his motivation, we will hear someone who sincerely wanted to help Job give up a sinful attitude toward God. We will hear him speaking as a friend to a friend, with the goal of helping his friend accept some hard truths and at the same time giving him comfort. (Note: Elihu addressed Job by name, something the three friends never did.)

Elihu began by repeating what he had heard Job say: He was guilty of no sin and God was afflicting him unjustly.

Elihu seems to have thought like Job's friends, that Job was committing a hidden sin. Elihu began with Job's claim that God was unfair. Those who say that God is unjust, Elihu said, and who demand that God give them a hearing and answer all their questions, are wrongly making themselves equal to God. (33:8-13)

God had not unjustly shut down the lines of communication. The fact that God chastens wayward believers proves that God is still speaking, even though it might not be the sort of communication we like. If the lines of communication are shut down, the fault is not with God. The fault lies with people, for they "do not pay attention to it" (Job 33:14).

People must listen to when and how *God* chooses to speak. God might speak

> In a dream, in a vision in the night,
> when people are falling into a deep sleep,
> while they slumber on their beds,
> he whispers a revelation into people's ears,
> and he confirms his warnings to them. (Job 33:15,16)

God's purpose in sending bad dreams is "to turn a man from his course of action and to suppress a person's pride" (Job 33:17). God wants to keep a person from suffering the consequences of their action: "He spares his life from the pit. He spares his life from crossing the stream of death" (Job 33:18). (33:14-18)

Or God may warn a person by sending suffering into their life: "Or a person may be *disciplined* on his bed by pain and by continual agony in his bones" (Job 33:19). Some say that Elihu was instructing Job about *chastening*. While the Hebrew word is often translated "chasten" (KJV, NIV), it can also be translated "rebuke" (ESV) or "reprove" (Young's Literal Translation) or "discipline" (as the EHV quoted above and others do). This is mentioned so that in our interpretation of Elihu's speech, we don't put too much emphasis on the particular word used in the English translation we are reading.

Elihu was describing in general how God communicates with people in the process of warning them against sin. Job's suffering and his restless nights (Job 17:13,14) was an instance of God's chastening activity. God was communicating with Job, but sadly Job was not paying attention, Elihu said.

Elihu then described what the suffering of chastisement leads to: "Then his soul draws near to destruction, and his life to those who bring death" (Job 33:22).

Elihu taught differently from Job's friends. Job's friends told him that his suffering was God's way of forcing him to give up his sins. They considered Job to be blessed that God was doing this to him. However their advice to Job quickly turned harsh when Job refused to accept it. They spoke as if God was simply giving Job what he deserved.

Elihu had a completely different purpose for talking about chastisement (or discipline). He did not tell Job what he should do for God but explained what God was doing for him.

Elihu spoke about a messenger who was able to serve as a mediator between Job and God. This mediator would bring the suffering person, who was about ready to die in his sins, to God's mercy. The mediator would say to God, "Spare him from going down to the pit. I have found a ransom for him" (Job 33:24). This description can fit only one person, God's messenger Jesus, the mediator between God and man who offered himself as a sacrifice to provide a ransom for all people and restore them to God. This is the same one whom Job called his Redeemer, or Protector, in Job's great statement of faith in chapter 19. (33:22-24)

If anyone accepted God's chastisement, repented, and believed what Elihu was saying about a mediator, they would be blessed once again. Their happiness would be restored:

> Then his flesh would become more vigorous than it was in his youth.
> He would return to days of youthful vitality.
> Then he would pray to God,
> and God would be pleased with him.
> With a joyful cry he would see God's face,
> and God would restore his righteousness to the man.
> (Job 33:25,26)

They would explain to others what had happened to them:

> Then the man would turn to people and say,
> "I have sinned, and I have perverted what is right,
> yet I was not punished as much as I deserved.
> God has redeemed my soul from passing into the pit,
> and my life will see the light." (Job 33:27,28) (33:25-28)

Elihu understood God's chastening activity, and he spoke well about God, as Job had done when he spoke about his Redeemer in chapter 19. (Job 19:25,26).

236

But at this point we face a problem. We are led to ask, "Was Elihu right to apply this to Job?" Elihu continued:

> Look, God does all these things with a man—
> two times, or even three times—
> to bring back his soul from the pit,
> so that light shines on him among the living.
> Pay attention, Job. Listen to me.
> Be silent, so that I may speak. (Job 33:29-31)

The friends had claimed that Job's suffering was brought on by his sins. Did Elihu do the same?

We can only answer, yes. We will explore this more fully in the special topic in this chapter. At this point, we'll simply note that although Elihu thought Job was sinning, his advice to Job was far different from that of the friends.

The friends impressed on Job that God gives us what we deserve. Elihu was impressing on Job that God does not give us what we deserve. Suffering was intended to lead a person to say, "I have sinned, and I have perverted what is right, yet I was not punished as much as I deserved" (Job 33:27).

The friends were harsh and became more belligerent toward Job as their speeches progressed, especially when in his third speech Eliphaz listed all the sins he thought Job had committed (Job 22:1-11). On the other hand, Elihu was kind toward Job, letting Job himself arrive at his own conclusion for why God was chastening him. In fact, Elihu told Job that they were both human beings, implying that he too needed to be chastened at times.

Yet Elihu and the three friends had this in common: They were acting in ignorance of everything God had said in the first two chapters about Job's innocence and about the reason for his suffering. They both addressed Job as an unrepentant sinner. (33:29-33)

Job 34 *Elihu's speech continues*

Elihu urged Job's friends to weigh their thoughts carefully before they spoke. (34:1-4) Elihu put Job's charge against God in a nutshell: Job said he did not rebel against God. He said that God was unjust for making him endure suffering he would never recover from. (34:5,6) Job derided God like the wicked do. Moreover, Job went so far as to say that since he kept God's commands but continued to suffer, then it made no difference whether he served God or not. (34:7-9)

At this point Elihu told Job how sinful he was for calling God unjust. Before we look at this, it is worth repeating that Elihu knew nothing about the reason why God was afflicting Job. He did not know that God had declared Job innocent. Nor did he know that God admitted he had destroyed Job "for no reason." He had likely never heard of Job's earlier unconditional acceptance of suffering without any talk of injustice on God's part.

Elihu carefully explained why he thought Job was wrong.

First, it is impossible, as Job claimed, for God to do anything wrong. "He repays a man for what he does. He causes the consequences of his ways to catch up with him" (Job 34:11). Elihu seemed to be saying the same thing as Job's friends. But as we saw, Elihu had already moved the focus away from God's justice and onto God's loving chastisement. (34:10,11)

Second, God is beyond criticism. He rules over all things. No one gave him that right; it was his for all eternity. His spirit gives life to all living creatures, and if he withdrew his spirit, all people would die. (34:12-15)

Third, no one who rules all things can be unjust. God governs all people impartially. He created all people, and "he shows no more regard for the rich than for the poor, because they are all the work of his hands" (Job 34:19). God knows what everyone does, and he punishes the wicked quickly and effortlessly. (34:16-21)

Fourth, there is no place for the evildoer to hide. God has no need to hold court to weigh the evidence. He knows what the wicked do as soon as they do it. When the innocent cry out, he destroys the wicked immediately. (34:22-28)

Fifth, Job had no right to criticize God's silence. God is not unjust if he refuses to answer our questions. If God wants to remain silent, he has the right to do so. Moreover, his silence does not mean that he has stopped acting justly. He continues to keep the powerful from oppressing the weak. (34:29,30)

Sixth, God wants people to repent of their sins and give them up. However, God is under no obligation to treat Job in the way Job was demanding. (34:31-33)

Considering God's control over all things, Elihu said, every understanding person would accuse Job of speaking wrongly by calling God's justice into question. Job is acting wickedly; he is rebelling against God; he shows contempt for God; and won't stop speaking words in criticism of God. Everyone agrees that God should be giving Job an even more painful test.

But again we must add, Elihu either did not know or he was overlooking the fact that for a long time Job had refused to call God unjust. It was only in the context of the arguments of Job's friends that Job accused God of treating him unfairly. Job was wrong, yes, but the history of Job's suffering was more complicated than Elihu realized.

How hard it is to support and comfort a suffering person when we don't have all the facts! (34:34-37)

Job 35 *Elihu's speech continues*

Elihu went further. He said to Job, "You even say, 'What use will this be to me? How will it profit me more than if I sinned?'" (Job 35:3). Job wondered what his righteous life had gotten him. He concluded that he might as well be wicked. That was not his firm position, but a statement made in weakness. In his final speech Job had said—and Elihu must have heard him say this—that he would to continue to follow God's will:

> Yes, as long as the breath of life is still in me,
> as long as the breath from God is still in my nostrils,
> my lips will not speak wickedness,
> and my tongue will not murmur deception.
> May I be cursed if I ever admit you are right.
> Until I die, I will never deny my integrity.
> I have held tight to my righteousness,
> and I will not let it go.

My conscience will not accuse me as long as I live.
(Job 27:3-6)

These were hardly the words of someone with a cavalier attitude toward sin, one who puts a wicked life on the same plane as a righteous life. (35:1-3)

Elihu returned to God's justice. Regardless of Job's views on a righteous and wicked life, nothing people do affects God. God is "self-contained," so to speak. Wickedness does not reduce his joy. Righteousness does not increase it. He can be impartial when he judges, not swayed by the affect his verdict might have on himself. What we do, Elihu said, only affects ourselves and those around us. (35:4-8)

Elihu pointed Job to what wicked people can expect from God. And Elihu had Job in mind. When they are afflicted, they cry out to God. But they are only looking for relief from suffering. None of them asks for the joy only God can give or the true wisdom that comes only from him. (35:9-11)

They cry out to God, but he does not answer. Why? Because their cries are insincere. They don't ask in humility but in arrogant pride. This was true for Job, Elihu claimed. Job had made his case before God, and now he was standing there, tapping his foot, waiting for God to answer. Elihu concluded, "Job opens his mouth pointlessly, and he heaps up words without knowledge" (Job 35:16). (35:12-16)

Job 36 *Elihu's speech continues*

God has a purpose for sending suffering into the lives of wicked people. He wants to warn them about the sinful course they are taking. In chapter 33, Elihu had explained this to Job in detail. If they repent, they will be blessed. But if they refuse, they will perish.

Along with that, they will have missed their chance to live in true wisdom—to wisely fear the Lord. Their suffering only makes them more angry with God. It does not lead them to repent. As a result, they die in shame. (36:1-14)

Elihu urged Job not to deal with chastisement like the wicked deal with it, but to accept it. Job should realize that "God delivers the afflicted by means of their affliction, and he gets their attention through their suffering" (Job 36:15). If Job repented, then God would restore the blessings he had taken from him. But by insisting on his innocence, Job was refusing to treat his suffering as God's loving chastisement. Job was acting like the wicked; therefore, he would continue to suffer.

Job should not allow anything to divert him from God's purpose; nor should he imagine that he could get out of his suffering on his own. He should not merely yearn for a time when he might be released. Rather, he should refrain from evil, which was why he was being chastened. (36:15-21)

Job had called God unjust. Elihu now described God's glory. He said to Job, "Listen to me. God is exalted in his power" (Job 36:22), and to that he attached the question:

Who is a teacher like him?
Who has dictated his way for him?
Who has said, "You have done wrong"? (Job 36:22,23)

Rather than criticize God for making him suffer, Elihu said, Job should "remember that you should praise his work, which people have celebrated in song" (Job 36:24). (36:20-25)

From here to the end of his speech, Elihu gave examples of God's glory, beginning with the fact that God is eternal. (36:26-33)

Job 37 Elihu's speech concludes

Elihu continued by describing God's power. Just thinking about it made Elihu tremble in awe.

He spoke of the thunder and lightning, the snow and rain, the cold winds of winter and the formation of ice. Rain clouds come with lightning, and they go wherever God wants: "Whether their purpose is to bring punishment or mercy to the world, he makes them achieve their goal" (Job 37:13). (37:1-13)

Only someone with "perfect knowledge" can do this, Elihu told Job (Job 37:16). You swelter when a hot south wind blows, and you have no power to make clouds moderate the heat. Trying to look at God's brilliance is like looking directly into the sun.

Elihu's speech ended on this note:

> As for the Almighty, we cannot comprehend him.
> He is exalted in power,
> but he does not violate justice and great righteousness.
> Therefore men should revere him,
> because he has regard for all those who are wise in heart.
> (Job 37:23,24) (37:14-24)

So ended Elihu's advice. He had turned Job away from the work-righteous religion of his friends. For that he substituted the scriptural teaching that God often chastens believers, leading them to repentance and to treasure the ransom that is stored up for them in heaven. He taught Job that repentant sinners can ultimately thank God and can tell others they have not gotten what they deserved.

~

Special Topic: Was God Chastening Job?

Throughout church history, many have agreed with Elihu that God sent suffering into Job's life to chasten (or discipline) him. Elihu, they say, provided Job with the answer he needed. This position has also been held by many in the Lutheran church.

Was Elihu correct? Did God afflict Job to chasten him—to lead him to recognize his sin, repent of it, and be forgiven? How we answer that question has a far-reaching affect on our interpretation. It will determine how we interpret all the speeches of Job. It will determine the overall meaning of Job and the lessons it intends to teach us.

Elihu said that God was making Job suffer so he, God, could get Job's attention and turn Job "from [his] course of action," "suppress [his] pride," and spare "his life from the pit" (Job 33:17,18).

Later in his speech, Elihu explained Job's suffering like this:

God delivers the afflicted by means of their affliction,

and he gets their attention through their suffering.
Certainly he is drawing you out of the jaws of distress
to a wide-open place, where you will not be hemmed in.
You will be comfortable at your table covered with rich
food.
But now you are caught up with the judgment of the
wicked,
and judgment and justice have taken hold of you.
(Job 36:15-17)

Because Job was rejecting God's chastisement, Job was experiencing "the judgment of the wicked," and God's "judgment and justice" had taken hold of him.

Was Elihu right? Was God chastening Job? That's the subject of this special topic.

The idea that God was chastening Job must be read into the text. There is no indication from the first two chapters or the last that God was chastening him. Elihu thought that Job was a sinner and that God was chastening him with suffering. God said that Job was blameless and innocent, a man who feared God and shunned evil. God said he was making Job suffer to disprove Satan's claim that Job's faith was insincere.

However, because of the prominence of the claim that Elihu was right and God was chastening Job, we'll look at the question more closely

Keeping Job's sins separate

The book of Job speaks about two sins: supposed sins of which his friends accused him but that he did not commit, and the sin that Job did commit when he called God unjust.

These two sins must be separated in order for us to be clear in our discussion. The supposed sin that led to Job's suffering must have started before Job's suffering began. This is the sin that Job's three friends had in mind when they accused him. Elihu, on the other hand, accused Job of calling God unjust. This is a sin that Job committed long after his suffering began. So it could not have been the reason for his suffering.

We begin by asking: For what sin did Elihu think that God was chastening Job? Was it because Job accused God of being unjust, or because Elihu—along with Job's friends—believed that Job had committed a sin that led to his suffering?

We will assume that Elihu understood the timing correctly. He realized that the sin for which God was chastening Job was not the sin that Job began to commit after his suffering began: the sin of calling God unjust. Nevertheless, Job's sin of calling God unjust was why Elihu rebuked Job in Job 32:2. And it was at the forefront of Elihu's words to Job in the rest of his speech.

Elihu summarized Job's accusation of God. Job said, "I am pure, without any sinful rebellion. I am clean. I have no guilt" (Job 33:9) and then he called God unjust, "But look how God finds pretexts to oppose me. He treats me like his enemy" (Job 33:10). Elihu replied, "Job, listen to this! You are not right. I must refute you! Why do you bring charges against him, just because he does not answer all of a man's questions?" (Job 33:12,13).

However, like the friends, Elihu believed that there must have been a reason for why God sent suffering into Job's life in the first place. The only difference between Elihu and the friends was their way of understanding God. The friends spoken wrongly about God and emphasized God's justice, while Elihu reflected the rest of Scripture when he spoke about God's love.

We might speculate that in Elihu's mind the two sins were both aspects of Job's spiritual state. Job was suffering because he had committed the sins his friends were referring to, and he was now challenging God's justice the way wicked people do.

Therefore, Elihu was right about Job's sin of accusing God of injustice. But along with Job's friends he was wrong in claiming that God was chastening Job for a sin he had committed that led up to his suffering

As we mentioned previously, like Job's three friends, Elihu did not know that God had called Job blameless and upright, a man who feared God and shunned evil, and that there was no one on earth like him. He did not know that God had destroyed Job for no reason found in Job. Elihu did not know that God—even now when Elihu was speaking to Job—considered Job his servant (Job 42:8), helping him prove that Satan was wrong.

Therefore, Elihu's claim that Job was being chastened—as accurate as was his description of God's chastening—was based on ignorance of the facts. It contradicted what God said about Job at the beginning of the book—that Job was blameless and upright. For these reasons we conclude that Elihu was wrong. God was not chastening Job.

At the end of Elihu's speech, Job said nothing. Some speculate that Job accepted Elihu's words and took them to heart. But there is nothing in the text that says that.

And there is another way to look at Job's silence, based on what the text of Job tells us. At the end of chapter 31, the writer said that Job's words had come to an end. To his friends he had repeatedly said: "I am not doing anything that deserves God's just punishment." That was the last thing he said before he concluded his speeches. What more could he have said to Elihu? His innocence answered the claim of his friends. It also would have been his answer to Elihu: "I am not doing anything to deserve God's chastening, even if he is chastening me in love."

Elihu gave Job a chance to respond to his analysis of Job's suffering. For example, at the beginning of his speech he said to Job, "Refute me if you are able. Lay out your case before me! Take your stand!" (Job 33:5). A little later he said, "If you have anything to say, answer me. Speak up, for I would be delighted to declare you innocent. If you have nothing to say, listen to me. Be silent, so I may teach you wisdom" (Job 33:32-33). But Elihu should have been observant enough to accept what Job said to his friends as Job's answer to him. But Job's words were finished. For Job to have repeated everything he said about his innocence was unnecessary.

Other ways to view Elihu's words to Job

Some interpret the matter differently.

1. Elihu said that Job's friends were wrong because there might have been other reasons why God was causing Job to suffer. Elihu offered chastening as a *hypothetical* example.

Of course, there *was* another reason for Job's suffering, namely, the contest between God and Satan. But might Elihu have used chastening as *a hypothetical example* of some other reason why Job might be suffering? In chapter 33 there is no hint that this was a hypothetical example. In Job 36:15-17, quoted above, Elihu repeated his description of chastening and applied it directly to Job.

2. God chastens people in view of a sin they *are likely to commit in the future to help them avoid it*

The idea is that God saw that Job was prone to call him unjust. So he brought suffering into Job's life in order to draw this sin out so he could correct it. However, this is a fictional idea. It runs against everything we know about Job and the stated reason why God afflicted him.

3. *The result* of the suffering determines *the reason* for the suffering.

Job *did* grow because of his sufferings. In the end, Job said he had heard about God, but now he had seen him. Also, Job saw how God vindicated him before his friends and before the entire world. And when James spoke about Job's perseverance, he mentioned the blessings Job received after it was over and used that to encourage all of us to persevere (James 5:11).

But must these outcomes define the purpose—even in part—for Job's sufferings? Theoretically, they might have. But there is nothing in the book of Job to suggest that they did, and everything the book says in the first two chapters points us in the opposite direction. Although positive things happened to Job because of his suffering, God's goal was to prove to Satan the power of his love and the genuineness of Job's faith. To suggest still other purposes is to read something into the book that is not there.

4. There are two kinds of chastening: chastening for a specific sin and chastening as a general sort of discipline.

The idea is that Job had not committed a special sin that needed God's chastisement, but that Job's sufferings were part of God's ongoing discipline to help Job mature in faith. This, however, is based on a distinction in the English language that is not present in the original Hebrew. The same Hebrew word translated "chasten" by some, is translated "discipline" by others. Older English translations use the first word while newer translations tend to use the second.

None of these attempts successfully interprets the book. God clearly tells us why he afflicted Job. God did not afflict Job because Job needed some spiritual blessing. It would be entirely counterproductive for God to have started the book of Job as he did if he intended it to conclude with chastisement as the answer to why Job was suffering.

What is the meaning of chastisement?

In English we often distinguish between punishment, chastisement, and discipline. Punishment is retribution for a crime, often with the intent of "rehabilitating" the offender. Chastisement is difficulty sent into a person's life to lovingly help that person give up a sin. Discipline is a more general, ongoing activity whose intent is to help a person grow in character and desire to live a more upright life.

Scripture makes these distinctions. But the distinctions are not reflected in various Hebrew words that have different meanings. Rather, the distinctions are based on the context.

Note Eliphaz's statement, "Consider this: How blessed is the man whom God corrects! Do not reject the *discipline* of the Almighty!" (Job 5:17). The Hebrew word here translated "discipline" in the English Heritage Version (EHV), which we are using, is the same word that other English versions translate "chasten." "Discipline" is used more often by newer translations while "chasten" is used by older translations. Both "discipline" and "chasten" are talking about the same thing, namely, God's work of "correcting" a person, as translated in the EHV version: "How blessed is the man whom God corrects" (Job 5:17).

In Job 33:19, Elihu uses yet another Hebrew word (yachah) to describe what he thinks God is doing to Job. This word too can be translated differently in English. The Evangelical Heritage Version (EHV) translates, "Or a person may be *disciplined* on his bed by pain and by continual agony in his bones" (EHV). For this verse, the Holladay Hebrew dictionary suggests the meaning "be admonished," and the Brown, Driver, Briggs Hebrew dictionary suggests "be chastened." The Evangelical Standard Version (ESV) uses "rebuke" with pain. Other versions use "be chastened" or "be disciplined."

Therefore, it cannot be said that although God was *not* chastening Job for a specific sin, he was disciplining Job in a more general sense. The Hebrew word does not make that distinction. The context must be our guide.

The first two chapters of the book rule out any goal suggested by the English words "chasten" and "discipline."

How the interpretation of Elihu affects the interpretation of the book of Job

Our interpretation of Elihu's solution greatly affects how we interpret Job. Here are some ways:

First, it affects how we interpret the prologue in chapters 1 and 2. The prologue clearly states the reason why God was afflicting Job. In chapter 2, after inflicting losses on Job, God described him as "a man who is blameless and upright, who fears God and turns away from evil. *And he still maintains his integrity*" (Job 2:3). This is not a description of a man who was resisting God's discipline. Moreover, as we have repeatedly pointed out, God said to Satan: "You incited me against him to destroy him *for no reason*" (Job 2:3).

Second, the idea that God was chastening or disciplining Job changes how we understand Job's statements of faith in Job 1 and 2. In those chapters, Job spoke about God's wisdom and his right to give or take away, and he praised God for what he had done. Today we use those statements as patterns of what every Christian should say in times of suffering or loss. But if God was chastening Job, then Job made those statements in ignorance or in willful denial of what God was really doing to him. In other words, if God was chastening or trying to correct Job, rather than accepting what God had sent into his life, Job should have been confessing his sins. That would have been the godly thing to do.

Third, Job's main argument to his friends was that he was innocent. Job asserted this throughout the entire conversation. He asked God to tell him how he had sinned. He asked God to examine his life, and he was confident that he could wear the results of that examination like a crown for everyone to see. He never expressed the thought that he might be doing something that brought on his sufferings.

Not only would Job have a completely mistaken view of his life of faith, but if Elihu was right and God was chastening Job, God would at the same time have been withholding from Job the very thing that would have ensured its success. He would have been withholding from Job the gift of insight to make Job aware that he was sinning and the awareness of what God was trying to accomplish by making him suffer. The reader would have to conclude that God was withholding that information from Job, waiting for Elihu to bring up the subject of chastisement and explain it to him.

Fourth, was Job so ignorant of what it meant to be chastened that he never considered it as the reason for his suffering so that he needed Elihu to explain it to him? God had said about Job: "There is no one like him on the earth, a man who is blameless and upright, who fears God and turns away from evil" (Job 1:8; 2:3). Was Job somehow different from every other believer so that he didn't need to be chastened from time to time when he drifted into sin. Did the words of Hebrews 12:7,8 not apply to him like they do to everyone else?

> It is for discipline that you have to endure. God is treating you as sons. For what son is there whom his father

does not discipline? If you are left without discipline, in which all have participated, then you are illegitimate children and not sons.

If all believers are chastened by the Lord, then Job also must have experienced God's chastening before. And if there was no one on earth like Job, the idea that he needed the young man Elihu to instruct him about the meaning of chastening—to explain its dynamic and its purpose—the idea of chastening should be carefully reconsidered.

Fifth, the idea that Job was rejecting God's attempt to chasten or discipline him leads us to question why Ezekiel included Job along with Noah and Daniel as examples of the most righteous of people (Ezekiel 14:14,20), and why James could use him as an example of Christian perseverance (or "steadfastness," as in the ESV) (James 5:11). In the latter case, if Job had been committing sins that needed to be corrected, his perseverance in the faith should have led him to acknowledge the correctness of Elihu's claim that God was lovingly chastening him. But the argument that his silence at the end of Elihu's speech shows that he agreed with Elihu is an argument from silence.

Sixth, one wonders if Elihu took into consideration the severity of Job's suffering. I am speculating somewhat, but it lines up with something God said through Jeremiah. In Jeremiah God said that the severity of his soon-to-come punishment on Judah should have indicated its purpose. Jeremiah wrote about the Lord's punishment on Judah like this:

At that time it will be said to this people and to Jerusalem, "A hot wind from the bare heights in the desert toward the daughter of my people, not to winnow or cleanse, *a wind too full* for this comes for me. Now it is I who speak in judgment upon them." (Jeremiah 4:11)

Couldn't Elihu sense that the hot wind blowing on Job was "a wind too full" to be a tool to "cleanse" Job? Consider all the people who died, all the possessions that were lost, and the severity of Job's physical suffering and its duration. Might not Elihu have sensed that perhaps something other than God's discipline was behind Job's suffering? The latter conclusion would have enabled Elihu to comfort Job better.

The idea that God was chastening Job sounds good on the surface. But if we project this idea backward and weigh it against everything we know about Job from the rest of the book, we realize it could not have been the reason for Job's suffering. God clearly said that Job was not suffering for something he had done. He was suffering for a reason known only to God, to Satan, and perhaps to the angels. God later rebuked Job for one sin only—the sin he committed during his time of suffering, namely, Job's accusation that he was unjust. Not only does this shape the way we interpret the book of Job, but it has tremendous application to how we comfort the suffering.

Elihu's place in the book of Job

If Elihu was wrong about Job, then what is his place in the book?

If Elihu had *not* been included in the book of Job, the book would still contain important lessons. For example, God does not always reveal his reasons for sending suffering. When helping others, we must avoid false accusations that can lead people into work-righteousness. We should help the suffering overcome the idea that God is unjust. We should bear patiently with the suffering person's rash words, urge them to accept what God has sent and let them know that he can bless them again.

But if the book had ended without Elihu, it would have been incomplete. Without Elihu, we would have learned only about the experience of a single man, Job, who at one point in his life was being made to suffer for no reason for which he needed to be chastened. God may send suffering into a person's life for a reason unrelated to chastening. In chapter 4 of this book we looked at Scriptural examples of suffering and saw that there are various reasons why God brings suffering into people's lives.

But chastisement (discipline) is, in fact, a prominent reason, and Elihu brought up that subject. We find nothing wrong in Elihu's speeches. Elihu, unlike Job's friends, fully understood God's love. He knew that God does not give us what our sins deserve. He spoke about a mediator in heaven who has prepared a ransom for us. He knew that people who have been chastened rejoice in what God has done for them.

He gave us the alternative to the friends' rigid and legalistic way of applying God's justice—which fueled Job's accusations against God and would have led Job to use good works to get God to end his suffering. He gave us Scripture's teaching about chastening, which is centered on God's love for his people. His teaching is one that all Christians can take to heart.

Elihu realized that there was an alternative to the friends' analysis of Job's suffering. But he didn't know all the facts. He had not heard God describe Job's innocence to Satan and Satan's counter challenge, which ultimately led to Job's suffering. Elihu was wrong to conclude that God was chastening Job.

For this reason, Elihu interpreted everything Job said as an attempt to avoid confessing his sin. Elihu said harsh, cruel things to Job, even classifying him among the wicked. He was wrong to do this. His words did not apply to Job.

But he was right about Job's serious sin of calling God unjust. Elihu's speech ended with an approaching thunderstorm, which suggested God's impending judgment on the sins for which Job refused to repent. If so, he was wrong about what God would say to Job. But his words provided a good starting point for what God *would* say.

Chapter 11

God Rebuked Job—Job 38–41

Getting Into the Book

Reading—Chapters 38–42

Job 38 *Verses 1-3*

God appeared to Job out of a whirlwind and confronted him.

Verses 4-41

Who are you, God began, to criticize my plans with your ignorant words? Let's see how much you know and how much power you have.

Where were you when I created the world, an act that brought joy to the angels?

Who created the sea and set boundaries to keep it from encroaching on the dry land?

Have you directed the sun to rise and set at the proper times? Have you controlled the wicked by making them flee the light and hide in darkness?

Have you surveyed the depths of the ocean? or gone through the gates of death? or explored the whole earth? If you have, tell me what you found.

Tell me where the light and darkness reside? Surely you know, for you have been around such a long time.

Where are the snow and hail kept, which I can use to control such things as the outcome of a battle?

Where are the lightning and wind kept? Who controls the floodwaters and the thunder, which cause plants to grow in unknown places where no one lives? Who gave birth to the rain, the dew, the ice, and the frost? Who turns the water rock hard?

Can you govern the stars in the sky or control dramatic natural events that happen on earth?

Can you supply people with wisdom and understanding?

Can you control the rain so it softens the earth?

Can you supply daily food to the lion, or to the raven, whose nest of chicks must be fed?

Job 39 Verses 1-30

Do you know when the animals give birth so you can watch over them?

Have you given the wild donkey a home in the desert, far from the noise of inhabited towns?

Can you harness the wild ox so it plows and does other tasks for you?

Have you created the ostrich, careless as it is about where it lays its eggs, but whose foolishness is compensated for by her strength?

Have you created the horse with its eagerness to join the battle? When the battle cry sounds, it fearlessly joins the charge.

Have you given the hawk its power to soar. Have you made the eagle able to live in the cliffs and given it eyesight keen enough to find food for its young even at great distances?

Job 40 Verses 1-5

Job, how can you dare make charges against me or correct my plans? If you want to accuse me, then state your case.

Job answered: I am far below you! I did accuse you, but I will not do so again.

Verses 6-14

Job, I have more to say. So get ready to answer me.

Will you really deny that I am just? Will you convict me of wrongdoing and make me defend myself? Are you as powerful as I am? Do you have divine dignity and honor? Is your splendor and majesty as great as mine?

Can you convict the wicked of sin? Can you humble them in your anger? Can you bury them in the dust? If you can, then I will praise you. I will admit that you have power to save yourself.

Verses 15–24

> Let's look at two creatures that I created, just as I created you.
>
> The first is behemoth. Consider his strength. His bones are like tubes of bronze or bars of iron. He is the most powerful of all my creatures. He makes his home in the water among the lotus plants surrounded by poplars. The wild animals play around him. When the stream floods, he is not afraid. Nor is he afraid when people try to capture him.

Job 41 *Verses 1–34*

> Or consider Leviathan.
>
> Can you capture him? Will he talk nicely with you? Will he agree to be your servant? Can you play with him or give him to your girls for a pet? Can you treat him like something you catch to sell in the marketplace?
>
> Can you hunt him with harpoons and spears? Just try. You'll be in a fight for your life, and you'll never do that again. Don't even think of capturing him. The sight of him will scare you to death. In fact, you don't even want to wake him up.
>
> Job, if I created such a beast, how can you think that I am unjust and must answer to you? Why, everything on earth belongs to me.
>
> Let me tell you more about Leviathan. He is designed for power. A person cannot remove his skin; it's like armor. No one can pry open his mouth. No one wants to get near his teeth. His back is

tightly closed up with shields, as it were. They are joined so closely that not even a breath of air can get through.

When he snorts, sparks of fire come out. His eyes are as bright as the sun rising in the sky. Smoke comes out of his nostrils. His breath can ignite coals. Fire comes from his mouth.

His neck is strong, and it terrifies anyone he chases. His flesh is solid and cannot be penetrated. Nothing can terrify him, and there is no one who is not terrified by him.

He is impervious to weapons. They snap like twigs. He is not afraid of arrows. Sling stones just bounce off him. Clubs do nothing. He just laughs at them.

His underbelly is protected by hard and sharp objects so that when he walks, he leaves a trail behind him.

He heats up the water when he swims. He churns up the deep, leaving a turgid wake behind him.

He is tall and looks down on the lesser creatures standing below him. He fears nothing.

Job 42 Verses 1-6

God's words led Job to confess his sin. He confessed his errors of questioning God and complaining about his suffering. He said:

You can do all things.

Nothing you do can be stopped.

You challenged me to defend myself for criticizing your plans. I didn't know what I was talking about. I was forming conclusions about things way over my head.

I wanted to question you about my sufferings but couldn't find you. Now you have revealed yourself to me, and you are the one asking the questions. All I can do is despise myself and repent for the ignorant way I spoke about you.

At that point God began to vindicate Job. We covered Job 42 in chapter three of the first part of this book when we established the guideposts for interpreting Job. If you wish, review the points made in that chapter. In brief, God said that Job had spoken about him correctly, that the friends had not spoken about him correctly, and they needed Job to offer sacrifices for their forgiveness. God vindicated Job's life to his friends and acquaintances, who visited him and gave him gifts. And God vindicated Job to the world by giving him three daughters, whose nobility and beauty surpassed that of all others; he restored everything he had taken away; and he gave Job a long life and many offspring.

Special Topic: God's Wisdom and Power

God rebuked Job by giving him a detailed description of his wisdom and power. He asked Job if he could do what God can do and if he could figure out why God does what he does.

But the theme of God's wisdom and power did not come up first in God's speech to Job. Everyone in the conversation had already spoken about God's wisdom and power. In fact, the longest section of their speech was often a description of God's power. On the surface, each person said the same thing. And they were correct. In fact, they said much the same as God said in his speech to Job.

But as we have seen, none of the people in the conversation knew why God was afflicting Job. Each was trying to give Job the wisdom he needed to understand and deal with his suffering. Job also was trying to understand his suffering even as he complained about God's unfairness. Although each of the three parties said much the same thing about God's wisdom and power, each spoke about him in the context of their own wisdom. The words may have been similar, but the context changed their purpose.

Before we look at God's own description of his wisdom and power, we'll look at how Job's three friends, Elihu, and Job spoke about it.

Job's friends. The friends offered a very straightforward analysis of Job's suffering and a simple answer to it. The friends believed that Job was getting what he deserved for some sin he was committing. God was trying to get Job to give up that sin. Then God would restore his blessings.

In that context, their use of God's wisdom and power was also very straightforward. God knew all things and he had infinite power to do what he wanted. He could easily take away a sinner's blessings and he could restore them just as easily.

The friends spoke about God's power to assure Job of God's complete control over his life. Eliphaz said, "For though he may inflict wounds, he also bandages them. Though he may strike, his hands also heal" (Job 5:18). If a person has sinned, is being punished by God, and then gives up that sin—which was what the friends were trying to get Job to do—God has full power to restore their fortunes.

In his first speech, Zophar rebuked Job for complaining against God, who is far above all human beings. He said,

> Can you explore the essence of God?
> Can you find a limit to the perfections of the Almighty?
> They are as high as the heavens. What can you do?
> They are deeper than hell. What can you know?
> His dimensions are greater than the earth
> and wider than the sea.
> If God comes and arrests someone and puts him on trial,
> who can overrule him?
> Certainly he recognizes deceitful men for what they are.
> He sees evil, and he recognizes it for what it is.
> (Job 11:7-11)

Zophar then offered Job the solution to his problems. If he appealed to God, he could be confident that God's wisdom and power would deliver him:

> But you, if you make your heart steadfast,
> and you spread out your hands to him,
> if you put away the sin you are holding in your hand,
> and you do not allow injustice to dwell in your tents,

266

> The rest of your life will be brighter than noon.
> Darkness will become like morning. (Job 11:13,14,17)

No one can escape God's limitless power and knowledge. Job could not hide his sin or flee God's judgment. Job could also trust God's limitless power and knowledge to restore his blessings if he repented and gave up his sin.

Elihu. Elihu's wisdom for Job was also straightforward. He said that Job was being chastened by God and Job should accept it. But unlike Job's friends, Elihu kept the spotlight on God's love. For that reason, even though his words were critical of Job, his talk about God's power can be read in the context of God's mercy.

Toward the end of his speech, as Elihu gloried in God's great wisdom and power, he said to Job:

> Watch out. Do not turn to evil,
> because that is why you have been tested by affliction.
> Listen to me. God is exalted in his power.
> Who is a teacher like him?
> Who has dictated his way for him?
> Who has said, "You have done wrong"?
> Remember that you should praise his work,
> which people have celebrated in song.
> All mankind has observed it.
> People can look at it from a distance.
> Yes, God is exalted far beyond our comprehension.
> The number of his years is beyond investigation.
> (Job 36:21-26)

Elihu continued with several more verses in which he described God's control over all the forces of nature.

Although these words contained a strong rebuke, Job could listen to them in the context of God's love—not just God's justice—which Elihu explained to him at the beginning of his speech. Coming from Elihu, these are words of hope based on God's forgiveness.

Job. The three friends had drawn Job into their world. They insisted that God was punishing Job. As long as he was in the world of his friends, the combination of his suffering and God's greatness put up an insurmountable wall between him and God and made him wary of being in God's presence.

Job knew that God was far greater than him. In 9:5-13 Job gave a wonderful description of God's greatness. But if his friends were right and his suffering was a punishment from God, God's greatness and power were to be feared. Job yearned to have a conversation with God: "I want to match words with him, but even if I am in the right, I cannot answer him" (Job 9:14-15).

Job knew that God was far above him in strength: "If it is a question of strength, he definitely is the strong one." He knew that God's court was the highest in the universe: "If it is a question of jurisdiction, who can summon him?" (Job 9:19). Job boldly wanted to approach God to discuss his case. But after confessing God's power, he told his friends what such boldness might cost him:

> Silence! Let me speak.
> I intend to speak up, no matter what happens.
> Even if he slays me, I will wait for him with hope.
> No matter what, I will defend my ways to his face.
> (Job 13:13,15)

Job thought that his suffering, sent by the powerful and all-knowing God, was insurmountable proof of God's anger. In one place Job asked God to remove his suffering for a while so they could talk:

> Just do two things for me, God.
> If you do, I will not hide from your face.
> Take your hands off me,
> and do not terrify me with your grandeur.
> Summon me, and I will answer.
> Or, I will speak, and you can respond to me.
> (Job 13:20-22)

But the real Job—God's new creation—did not live in the world of his friends. At the beginning of his suffering, he would not let God's great wisdom and power frighten him. He accepted whatever God gave him and he refused to interpret his suffering as punishment.

And toward the end of his speeches, he proclaimed God's greatness with praise unmixed with fear. He said,

> He stretches out the northern sky across the emptiness.
> He suspends the earth on nothing.
> He encloses water in his clouds,
> but the clouds are not broken apart by its weight.
> He dims the face of the full moon by veiling it with his clouds.
> He drew a circle around the surface of the waters.
> It marks the boundary of light and darkness.
> The pillars of the heavens shake.
> They are stunned by his rebuke.
> By his power he calmed the sea.
> By his understanding he smashed Rahab.
> By his breath the skies became beautiful.

> His hand pierced the fleeing serpent.
> But all these are just the fringe of his ways!
> How faint a whisper we hear of him!
> Who understands his power, which is displayed in the
> thunder? (Job 26:7-14)

Many say that Elihu's words at the end of his speech naturally led into God's speech about his divine wisdom and power. Due to the closeness of Elihu's concluding words and God's speech, that may be true. However, an argument could also be made that the above words of Job could serve as an introduction to God's speech, and perhaps do a better job of it. Elihu's praise of God's perfect wisdom and power were one aspect of his chastening activity. Job's words, however, were a pure hymn of praise to God. As words spoken by someone who knew he was suffering under God's power, they were pure praise to God, not a component of some larger system of wisdom.

God. The entire conversation between Job and his friends, including Elihu's words about chastening, were colored by the question, why? The friends thought they knew why God was afflicting Job—that God was afflicting him because of his sin. Elihu also thought he knew why—that God was chastening him because of his sin. In times of weakness, Job had wondered why God was afflicting him and he accused God of acting unjustly. But none of them had been in heaven to learn the real reason for Job's suffering—an act of God that has proved the greatness and power of his love and promises to all generations since.

God's speech was intended to lead Job—and us—to stop asking why. God's rebuke of Job was nothing more than a description of himself. That was all. God did not weave his description of himself into some overarching principle that people can use to figure out why he might be afflicting them or what they might do to cause their suffering to stop. God's description of his creation and governance of the world—this powerful description of his knowledge and power—was the sum total of the wisdom he wanted Job to think about. God wanted Job simply to confess that God had already figured his life out for him, and that everything was in order. God's description of himself is true wisdom. It is the only thing that frees us also from the temptation to think that God is unjust. It enables us to stop asking why, to put our trust in him, to fear him, and to shun evil.

When his suffering began, Job said that God had the right to give and to take away, to send bad things as well as good. He did not know why God was making him suffer, but he continued to praise God and maintain his integrity. After God's speech, Job took up that attitude again. God's words to Job lead us also to imitate Job's attitude. God knows why he shapes our life as he does. That is our wisdom, and it is all we need.

⋙

Looking at Job

Job 38-42:6 *God rebukes Job*

God rebuked Job for one thing only: In the latter days of his suffering, when pressed by his friends to think

that God was afflicting him because of his sin, Job
had said he had done nothing wrong and that God
was unjust. God rebuked him for that particular sin by
impressing on him the power and wisdom with which
he made the world and continues to govern it. Job
repented for the sin of questioning God's ways, which
was what God wanted him to do.

At this point it's refreshing that we don't have to sort
out what's right and what's wrong in a speech. In
God's speech, everything was right. We won't go into
more details about that speech. The summary of God's
words at the beginning of this chapter will serve as our
overview of the content of what he said to Job in Job
38–42:6.

Chapter 12

Comforting Job

Wisdom to comfort

All people are affected by suffering, either in their own lives or in the lives of people around them. While some people are calloused and refuse to help those who suffer, in others there beat hearts of compassion and the desire to help. We are thankful for that, and we pray that we are blessed by such people when God brings suffering into our lives.

From Job's complaints, we learn that his illness drove many away. But there were still a few who wanted to help comfort him. The four people who tried to comfort Job all believed in God and knew many things about him. They thought they could help him endure suffering in a God-pleasing way. To do this, they tried to help Job make sense out of his suffering, and find an answer to how Job could escape it.

But did they have the wisdom to do so? The book of Job is not so much about suffering per se. It is about how God wants us to respond when suffering comes into our lives or into the lives of others—especially how we respond to God, the one who is in control of every aspect of our lives. To be comforters we must find the wisdom to do that. This is what the book of Job helps us do.

Comforting others is not, as they say, rocket science. It does not require a theological degree or a technical course in counseling. If we accept the fact that God has our lives figured out even though we don't, and if we understand God's plan of salvation as taught in Scripture, we cannot but be good comforters of the Jobs who come into our lives.

The rest is common sense. If your heart is filled with God's grace in Christ, it will be easy to get it right. If what you say to yourself gives you hope, it will likely give others hope. If what you say makes you feel guilty, it will likely make them feel guilty too. This applies not only to what you say but also to how you say it and when you say it.

This summary chapter will help us pull together some lessons from the book of Job on how to comfort others. To do that, we will look at what Job and the other people in the book believed and how this influenced what they said. First, we'll review what they were thinking. Second we'll draw some lessons from what they said.

First, we will quickly summarize their thinking as they struggled to respond to Job's suffering.

The friends. The friends knew that God is wise and powerful, that he knows all things and always does what is right. He always punishes the wicked and blesses the righteous.

Since you are being punished, they told Job, it is a sign that you are committing a sin and that you are refusing to give it up. You might have deceived people in the past, but you can't deceive God.

Nevertheless, God is giving you a way out of your suffering, they said. Since his justice is making you suffer, his justice will also take your suffering away. So put away your sins. God will remove your suffering and replace it with health, and he will restore to you everything he has taken away.

The friends, however, were not speaking correctly about God. They showed little understanding of God's love and his promise of a Savior. They did not know how to bring God's mercy into their advice. Their wisdom was the wisdom of the world, which always leads to the idea that people must earn God's favor. This made it impossible for them to comfort Job.

Elihu. Elihu knew the friends were wrong for concluding that Job was a sinner because God was afflicting him. They had never identified what sins Job was committing. Elihu also knew that Job was wrong for saying that God was unjust.

Elihu understood God's mercy and he knew that all people have a mediator before God. And so, he could speak wisely. He told Job that God was speaking to him through sufferings. Therefore, Job's suffering did not originate from God's justice, but from his love. If you would but listen, Elihu told Job, you would hear God telling you to repent of your sins and serve him wholeheartedly.

Elihu thought that God was chastening Job like a
parent chastens a child. If Job took God's chastening
to heart and gave up whatever he was doing wrong, he
would find joy in God's presence. Elihu told him, "Your
mediator will tell you about the ransom that he has
given you, and you will be confident of God's forgiveness. You will tell others that even though you sinned,
you did not get what your sins deserved.

He urged Job to recognize God's power and wisdom
and accept his chastisement.

Job. Job knew he was a sinner like all people, and
he offered sacrifices for the forgiveness of sins. He
respected and loved God, and he lived in the light of
God's love and forgiveness.

God gave him great blessings. But he took them all
away and afflicted him with a horrible disease. Job continued to praise God and acknowledge that he had the
right to do whatever he wanted. And he confessed that
God had the right to send him good things and bad
things.

Job resolved never to give up his integrity. Nor would he
ever deny that he was blameless and innocent because to
deny that would be to deny God whose love and mercy
had prompted him to live that kind of life.

Accordingly, Job would never admit that he was suffering because he was a sinner, as his friends claimed.
Yet as the suffering wore on, Job's appreciation of God's
love began to erode under the influence of his friends'
emphasis on God's justice. Job began to wonder why
God in the past had shown him his power by blessing
him, but suddenly began using his power to afflict him.

Job knew that he had feared God and shunned evil, and was still doing that. He couldn't avoid concluding that God was afflicting him for not reason, that God was unjust and arbitrary. God's wisdom and power used to comfort him. But in view of his suffering, God's wisdom and power made him afraid of God.

Job wanted to argue his case with God, but he couldn't find him. And even if he did, Job was afraid of how God might react.

But no matter what was happening to him, Job knew that he had a Redeemer in heaven, a Goel, whom on the last day he would finally see with his own eyes. His Goel—who was God himself—would argue his case in his own courtroom and he himself would testify to Job's sincere faith and innocent life.

His friends accused Job of sin, and his suffering seemed to prove they were right. But he would never deny his faith or abandon the life he was living for God.

God. God had always dealt graciously with Job, comforted him with his presence, and given him many blessings.

But at a certain point in Job's life, God wanted to use Job to prove something to Satan. He wanted to show Satan the power of his love, which had elicited such loyalty from Job. He wanted to use Job to show Satan that it doesn't take an outpouring of physical blessings to win a person's love. His forgiving love and his promise of a Savior was enough.

In order to prove the sincerity of Job's faith and dedication, God took away everything he had given him and made his life unbearable with suffering.

Moreover, God turned his face away from Job and left him to struggle on his own, using only the strength provided by his faith in God's Word. Would that alone be enough to enable Job to persevere? Would that alone enable him to resist all human logic about the reason why he was suffering? Would he be able to withstand the temptation to curse God as Satan said he would? Those were the questions Job's losses and suffering were meant to answer.

Job sinned against God by calling him unjust. And God had to rebuke Job. Job accepted God's rebuke. Throughout it all, Job persevered in faith and remained God's servant. For thousands of years Job has served as God's example of a person who persevered because of his hope in God's salvation.

Out of the abundance of the heart the mouth speaks

Jesus said, "The good man brings good things out of the good stored up in his heart . . . . For out of the overflow of his heart his mouth speaks" (Luke 6:45). Our appreciation of God's forgiveness in Christ and our knowledge of his mercy will fill our hearts so we can be God-pleasing comforters.

Some lessons from the book of Job

The book of Job is a search for wisdom. Job's sufferings prompted a debate about the wisest way the people in

Job's life could comfort him. For us, the book prompts us to search for wisdom to comfort the Jobs in our lives.

The wisdom of the friends centered on God's justice. They were right about God's justice. But they did not know God well enough to use the fact of his justice to comfort Job. Their wisdom was the wisdom of the world, which is built on the human sense of God's justice but is devoid of God's love in Christ. It would lead Job to foolishly embrace work-righteousness.

Elihu wisely understood that God often chastens his children. But from Elihu we learn that it is not wise to assume why a person is suffering, even though it might be Scripturally true and apply in many cases. Elihu's wisdom would have led Job to foolishly deny his integrity that had been inspired by his knowledge and love for God. We must realize that all believers have been serving God and must never give them reason to deny that fact.

From Job we learn that wisdom is to live in the fear of the Lord—to believe his promises and dedicate our lives to his service. This is true wisdom. But we should not be surprised if we hear a suffering person accuse God of injustice, like Job did.

From God we learn that wisdom is to say to him, "You are God, and I am not." Wisdom is to confess that his ways are perfect even when his reasons are hidden from us—even when what he does runs counter to what we might rightly claim is just. Wisdom is to honor, love, and serve him at all times and in all situations. And from what God did for Job after his suffering was over, we learn that whether on earth or in heaven, God will

279

free us from our suffering, vindicate our faith, and richly bless us.

Thoughts on applying these lessons to ourselves and to others.

When we search for wisdom to counsel others, we learn from the book of Job that all such wisdom does not come from a particular book, even from the book of Job. Although the book of Job gives us many truths, gaining wisdom is largely a matter of growing to know the blessings God has given to us—blessings that comfort us whether we are suffering or not.

Specifically, it is to know Christ. It is to have Paul's prayer to God more and more fulfilled in our own lives:

> For this reason I bow my knees before the Father, from whom every family in heaven and on earth is named, that according to the riches of his glory he may grant you to be strengthened with power through his Spirit in your inner being, so that Christ may dwell in your hearts through faith—that you, being rooted and grounded in love, may have strength to comprehend with all the saints what is the breadth and length and height and depth, and to know the love of Christ that surpasses knowledge, that you may be filled with all the fullness of God. (Ephesians 3:14-19)

As we grow in the knowledge of the breadth and length and height and depth of God's love in Christ, the more that love will shape how we comfort others.

So the main thing we can do to become better counselors is to immerse ourselves more in the Word of God. Whether that is in public worship, Bible study, family

Bible reading or personal Bible reading, the Holy Spirit will be working in our hearts, fulfilling Paul's request to God for us. Then our mouths will speak naturally out of the overflow of our hearts.

Ask God to help you share your Christ-centered wisdom with the suffering. In Romans 12, Paul lists several spiritual gifts. Among them are the gifts of exhortation and showing mercy (Romans 12:8). Perhaps God has given you those special gifts already. But if he has given you other gifts, there is nothing wrong with asking him to give you those gifts also so you can better deal with suffering.

Ask God to enable you to exhort others—to listen when you have nothing to say and to speak wisely so that what you say builds up the suffering person in the hope given by God's forgiving love.

Comforting others is sometimes difficult to do, as are all acts of showing mercy. Ask God to give you a desire to build up the suffering person in the knowledge of God's mercy. Ask that he help you find joy in doing so—that he give you a spirit made cheerful by the Gospel.

Have a few of your favorite passages at hand—passages from which you get comfort. Commit them to memory, or perhaps the important phrases, so you can quickly use them at an appropriate moment. Here are a couple.

In Psalm 103 the psalmist writes,

> The LORD is compassionate and gracious,
> slow to anger, abounding in love.
> He will not always accuse,
> nor will he harbor his anger forever;

he does not treat us as our sins deserve
or repay us according to our iniquities.
(Psalm 103:8-10 NIV84)

Or think of what Asaph said in Psalm 73 while going
through suffering:

Yet I am always with you;
you hold me by my right hand.
My flesh and my heart may fail,
but God is the strength of my heart and my portion
forever.
(Psalm 73:23,26 NIV84)

Choose your own favorites. Mark them as they come up
in your Bible reading

Some lessons from Job's three friends

We see how important it is for us to center our thoughts
on Christ. That is where the friends failed. The friends'
advice to Job was not completely devoid of God's love
(note Eliphaz's statement in Job 5:17). However, most
of what they said came from their emphasis on God's
justice. Their emphasis on God's justice resulted in leading Job in a number of directions. It led Job to doubt
God's forgiveness, which he did; to be afraid of God,
which he sometimes was; to give up serving God out of
love and think he had to become a more moral person
to earn back God's favor, a deadly sin Job avoided; and
to tempt him to criticize God's wisdom and justice,
which is what God rebuked him for.

These are things that you, as a comforter, ought never
lead a suffering person to do.

The friends' justice-based (actually, law-based) counseling was easy. But when God's love—his promise of forgiveness through the Savior—is at the heart of your Christian counseling, then it becomes tricky to say the right thing, because you are working to combine God's justice and mercy.

Use what God has said in his Word about his justice—he will punish the wicked. Use that fact as a warning if you think the suffering person needs it. But realize that God's mercy in Christ is the only truth that can strengthen a suffering person. That must be at the center of the comfort we give just at it is at the center of everything we do as God's children. Acceptance should predominate, not implications—overt or subtle—that the suffering person is getting what he or she deserves. The good news in Christ must always be present lest the suffering person think that since they are suffering, God has not forgiven them.

Help them if they are resorting to good works to make their suffering end. On the other hand, also help them if they are dismissing God's justice. Sometimes it is hard to know exactly what you should say. But you must decide the best thing to say, and that is why the state of your own heart is so important. Lutherans often say that the most difficult part of advising others is to know when to speak the Law and when to speak the Gospel. How true that is! But when your own heart is fortified by the Gospel, you will know which one to speak. When you daily repent of your sin, you know when to talk about God's Law—his justice or his use of chastisement. And when you do that, you will naturally be directing the suffering person to hope in Christ.

If you find yourself in doubt about what to say, it might be best to put off that discussion for another time—when you are more sure of which direction you should go.

Be aware that your suffering friend may be infected by the wisdom of Job's friends and may be applying that wisdom to themselves—making them doubt God, question his justice, or think in work-righteous terms. Don't be surprised if you encounter this. If so, explain the right way of thinking about God and help the person know that true comfort is found only in Christ's forgiveness.

At first you may find yourself offering general words of sympathy. But even at the first visit, try to offer the one truth—the message of God's forgiveness in Christ—that can provide comfort for their souls. And it is always wise to let the suffering believer express to you the reason for their hope to you rather than the other way around. To that end, be patient. Meet with a suffering Christian expecting to be strengthened yourself. With that attitude, your presence will be appreciated.

Some Lssons from Elihu

Elihu understood that God lovingly disciplines his children like parents discipline theirs. He knew that God can use suffering to help his wayward children more and more live lives of repentance and faith. Elihu wanted to help Job know this truth so Job could have the joy that comes from living in God's pardon.

Elihu was correct to rebuke Job for calling God unjust. However, when Job accused God of making him suffer for no reason, Elihu refused to entertain the thought that Job might be right, and that God was not afflicting him to chasten him. With no behind-the-scenes knowledge of why God was afflicting Job, Elihu could only guess.

Christians today can learn from him. A suffering Christian may divulge to you a sin they are committing and express guilt and the desire to give it up. In that case, Elihu provides a good outline to follow as you comfort that person: talk about sin and repentance. Start with contrition before God—not with feeling bad about sin, but with the fact that God will punish all sin. Then talk about their mediator in heaven, who has provided a ransom to free all people from the penalty of sin. Then tell them about the joy a forgiven sinner has when they realize that God has not given them what they deserve.

But before you make use of that outline, be sure it applies to the one you are trying to comfort. The person may hint that it does. Or you may have a concrete reason to think so. If so, don't be afraid to explain the meaning of God's chastisement.

But if you are not sure, then don't assume that God is chastening them. Don't force a confession out of them like Elihu tried to do with Job. Comfort them with the Gospel, because if they have sinned, the Gospel will strengthen their faith and prompt them to open up about a sin they may have committed. This will guide you in what to say. Trust that if God is chastening that person, he will also be leading them along the path to take his chastening to heart.

We all want to be in control of the situation—to have wisdom to offer the correct explanation. But be careful of doing that. Job's friends and Elihu wanted that form of control—the friends through their teaching of God's justice and Elihu with the teaching of chastisement. But comforters don't have that luxury. We should never presume to understand why the Lord is doing a particular thing to a particular person. Perhaps God is chastening that person. Perhaps not. Is it possible to tell the difference between when a person is suffering because they are not following God's will and when they are suffering because they are following God's will? The book of Job says no.

There is another situation you might face. The suffering person might have been taught something about God's chastisement but is unclear about it. They might suggest that because they are suffering, they must be doing something that is prompting God to purify them. If so, respond in a way that leads to comfort, not to blame. Don't be afraid to ask: "Can you really be sure about that?" Give them time to think it over. Perhaps they may reconsider. On the other hand, remember that God does use suffering to help Christians put off sin and grow in Christian maturity. That may, in fact, be what your suffering friend needs to hear.

If you help a Christian realize that God is chastening them, however, don't think that you and your friend have successfully probed the mind of God. God's reason for chastening his people and his ways of doing it are far more complex and hidden than Elihu seemed to think.

Even if we rightly conclude that God is chastening a suffering person, how many unanswered questions remain? Why is a person's suffering so severely? Does repentance immediately make suffering cease? After all, many forms of suffering never truly come to an end in this life. Why might other innocent people have suffered so much in what God was doing on our behalf? Can we spot the difference between when God is chastening a person for a specific sin and when in a more general way he is simply helping that person serve him more single-mindedly? Why does God not chastise others who have sinned? Why does God use blessings, not suffering, to lead some people to repent and give up sin? You have likely had other questions like these come up when trying to comfort others. Always remain aware that God's ways are most often hidden, and we must simply trust that he knows best. We never have the complete answer to suffering and this keeps us humble.

There is also the danger of thinking that those who don't suffer have no sins for which God needs to chasten them. This is a work-righteous idea and might come up.

Ask God for wisdom. If God is chastening the suffering person and wants you to be part of his chastening process, he will make it happen. Before you jump in with your solution, however, listen carefully to the suffering person. Neither Job's friends nor Elihu listened to Job. Elihu did invite Job to speak, but that was only after he had explained to Job in no uncertain terms the reason for his suffering. Ask God to move the conversation in the best possible direction. Give yourself time to choose the right words. Give the suffering person time to sort things out.

And in all cases, if the suffering person is an unbeliever, proclaim your hope in Christ even as you offer simple, human comfort.

Some lessons from Job

Over the years, Job had counseled many people. Based on his own initial reaction to the suffering God brought into his life, it is not hard to figure out how he likely counseled them. He would have talked about the Savior God promised. He would have pointed out the reasons why they could be confident in God's unfailing mercy and concern for them. Job would have said that we should praise God for everything that happens to us. He would have encouraged suffers to know that God gives and God takes away for his own reasons—not always for reasons we can understand. He also would have encouraged them never to give up their hope or stop serving God. This is true wisdom, and it filled Job's heart with everything he needed to give comfort.

The wisdom of his friends, however, seriously challenged Job's wisdom. Their teachings made Job question God: Is God really just? Is God really listening to me? When we hear Job wrestle with these questions, we see where the friends' false teaching was leading him, and where it always leads if Christian comforters focus one-sidedly on God's justice rather than on God's love.

When we look at Job, we realize that believers love God for who he is, not for how pleasant he makes their lives. God's forgiveness and love at work in a believer's heart has far more power to help them to persevere in faith than suffering has power to cause them to give it up. Even in times of suffering, that power is at work in the

Christian you are comforting, just like it was in Job's heart. This is your greatest ally. Expect your Christian friend to express their hope, and then rejoice because your Christian friend has just comforted you.

Also realize that Christians have a sinful nature, which may give rise to complaints. The Christian may even speak directly against God like Job did, calling him unfair or arbitrary. That doesn't mean the person has fallen from faith and should be treated as an unbeliever. Strengthen them by reminding them of the Savior.

In some cases, it might be good to remind them of the question God asked Job: "Where were you when I laid the foundation of the earth?" (Job 38:4). Don't be afraid to ask that question or one of the others God asked Job, and don't be afraid that the suffering person will reject you. Job didn't reject God. He took to heart God's rebuke and immediately applied it to himself.

In one of his speeches, Job said that he would even help those who were not believers. Take Job's words to heart. Unbelievers are fellow human beings and deserve our mercy too. Offer general words of comfort as you are able. Keep in mind that you can help them the most by giving them the hope of forgiveness and eternal life.

Often the best way to comfort others is to listen, which is one of the things Job yearned for. The friends didn't listen. From the start, they had it all figured out. Elihu didn't listen either. He offered to listen, but it was only after he reached his conclusion about Job.

As we mentioned before, people like to be in control of the situation and have *the* answer to a person's suffering. Or at least they want to have some insight, some specific advice, to share with their suffering friend. But we should remember that when we think about the "why" of suffering, we enter into the area of God's hidden wisdom, where we must let God be God.

We sometimes think we *must* have something to say, so we say things like, "Remember, God is doing this for your good" or, "You will learn from this how best to comfort others" or, "This will help you grow in your own faith." These truths are found in Scripture. But don't feel you are not doing your job if you just listen. A suffering Christian may be served best by your simple presence. Rely on God to give you wisdom and ask the Holy Spirit to give you the most helpful words to speak.

The most important lesson comes from God.

"Why am I suffering?" Job wanted to know. "Why won't you tell me?" Job asked God. God did not satisfy Job with answers to those questions. But he gave Job the one answer Job needed to hear—the one answer all Christians need to hear.

God began by rebuking Job for calling him unjust. God then told Job about divine wisdom. Divine wisdom is just that—it's divine, not human. God's wisdom cannot, nor should it, be probed by the human mind. All we have is the wisdom God has revealed to us in Scripture. God's revelation centers on truths about his just punishment on sin and his salvation in Christ. These truths revealed in Scripture enable us to live in the fear of the Lord.

As we saw in chapter 4 of this book, Scripture describes many times when God sent suffering. In some cases he does not reveal why. In some cases, he does. For example, God punished the Israelites for their sins after they left Egypt. After listing occasions when they sinned and when God punished them, Paul said, "Now these things happened to them as an example, but they were written down for our instruction, on whom the end of the ages has come" (1 Corinthians 10:11-12)

We know the reason for the flood, for David's loss of the child that was born to Bathsheba after his adulterous relationship with her and for the illnesses suffered by the Corinthians for misusing the Lord's Supper. These accounts warn us against sin. We apply them in a natural way to ourselves and to our fellow Christians. We wisely apply them in a general way, knowing that God uses or withholds punishment and chastening as he knows best. We don't willy nilly apply these accounts to current accounts of suffering where we have no insight into God's thoughts and plans.

When we try to understand the specifics of God's work in our lives, it is wise to maintain the attitude David expressed in Psalm 131:

> My heart is not proud, O Lord,
> my eyes are not haughty;
> I do not concern myself with great matters
> or things too wonderful for me.
> But I have stilled and quieted my soul;
> like a weaned child with its mother,
> like a weaned child is my soul within me.
> O Israel, put your hope in the Lord both now and forevermore. (Psalm 131:1 3 NIV84)

When we comfort others with God's revealed wisdom and avoid questions that lead us into matters that he has not revealed to us, we do well.

God gives and *God* takes away. To help others, it is important to clear up muddy thinking on that topic—in your own mind and in the mind of the sufferer. You need not enter into a theological discussion of this truth. Calm and clear statements injected into the conversation—which point out that God is the source of everything that comes into our lives—are often enough. When people know that God is the source of suffering, they will know where to turn for relief and for strength to persevere in faith.

It's likely that neither you nor the suffering person will ever figure out what God is doing when he sends suffering. Sometimes there is a reason, and in our opinion the reason is clear. But it's only our opinion and not one we have a right to force on another person. Sometimes there are hints at what God might be doing. But even then, we will never know the depth of God's plans and purposes. And very often—which is the hardest to accept—his perfect ways run counter to what is just and fair. But by faith we accept that they are.

Two examples of giving comfort from the book of Job.

We learn lessons from the book of Job, but no one can tell you how to offer comfort. If God has given you the task of comforting a friend, then he knows that you are the right person to do it. You know your friend, and your friend knows you. Ask God to give you wisdom to say the right thing at the right time.

Here are two scenarios from my own experience when I used the book of Job to comfort and counsel Christians who were suffering.

Dorothy. At a congregation I served, we had an arrangement with some local nursing homes. We offered to visit people whom no one else visited and who would be willing to listen to a couple chapters from Scripture each month.

One of the people I served was Dorothy. When I began visiting her, it was explained to me that she had been a healthy, active young girl. When she was seven, however, she was bit by a species of fly that almost completely paralyzed her. Her development had been stunted, and she had lain on a gurney for 30 years.

During the time I knew her, I read several books of Scripture to her, but Job wasn't among them. Finally, I decided to read it. I explained the nature of the book to her, and she wanted to hear it. So we started. I wondered how she would receive it, but I shouldn't have had any concerns. It spoke directly to her. Other than to indicate yes and no, she could only get out a few words. It was impossible for us to have a conversation. But as we read, she would groan. The groans came from deep within her, and they came at places in the reading I did not expect. It was clear to me that Dorothy truly understood the book of Job and understood it far better than I did.

Sometimes it is hard to know exactly what to say to a suffering person. With Dorothy, who was a Christian, it was easy. I couldn't communicate with her, but the

Scriptures we read spoke for themselves. We both knew how much she was suffering, but I didn't bring up the topic except in a general way in the context of forgiveness and the hope of eternal life. Talk of punishment would have been completely out of place. And in her case, talk of chastisement would have been cruel. She only needed to hear what Christ had done to save all people from their sins and give us the hope of eternal life.

After finishing Job, we started to read Philippians. A week after we heard Paul say, "For me, to live is Christ and to die is gain," the Lord ended her 32 years of lying paralyzed on a gurney. Perhaps the example of Job played a role in her final perseverance.

Harold. Harold was an older man. He lived alone in a trailer home. I met him through one of our members. After a couple visits, I asked him if he would like to take our church's Bible information class. We went through the class in his home. As we did, I came to realize what a remarkable past this unassuming man had had and just how intelligent he was. He joined our congregation. I don't think he was ever in our church, but I served him with regular visits.

One time I was a little late for our monthly visit. Harold had emphysema and he had gone on oxygen. He found it confining. He was quite miserable. As soon as I sat down, Harold lashed out with a long string of complaints against God: "Why has God done this to me? What have I done to deserve this? It's not fair."

After about 15 minutes of listening to that, without much thought—I had forgotten my Bible—I said,

"Harold, where's your Bible? He pointed to the shelf. I got the Bible, turned to Job 38, and read the whole four chapters in which God rebuked Job. I didn't look up as I read, fearing that he might be planning to show me the door. But when I finished and finally looked up, Harold was sitting there calmly. He simply said, "Thanks, I needed that."

Up to that moment in my visit I had not talked about God's forgiveness and the hope of eternal life. What Harold needed was a rebuke, like God gave to Job. And like Job, he took that rebuke to heart. I then realized how important it was that we had grown to know each other and that our relationship was centered on God's Word and Christ's forgiveness.

Doctors would administer medications to ease Dorothy's and Harold's pain. But neither the doctors nor I could comfort them by promising to make their lives easier. Nor can Christians promise that God will someday relieve the pain of a suffering friend and make their life easy, even though he has the power to do that.

But when we know that God's ways are always right, that his decisions are always wise, and that he always treats us as people whom he has forgiven—then we have the wisdom we need to comfort Job.

Appendix: Luther's Explanation of Job

A search was done on the "Job" index entry in the American edition of Luther's Works. Luther mentions various lessons Job can teach us. He often mentions Job when he is talking about God's chastisement or God's purification of his faith. This reflects a position held by most from the time of the ancient church. However, Luther's more extended treatments of Job speak differently.

Below is Luther's short introduction to the book of Job:[7]

The book of Job deals with the question, whether misfortune comes from God even to the righteous. Job stands firm and contends that God torments even the righteous without cause other than that this be to God's praise [after 1534, editions add], as Christ also testifies in John 9:3 of the man who was born blind.

To be sure, when Job is in danger of death, out of human weakness he talks too much against God, and in his suffering sins. Nevertheless, Job insists that he has not deserved this suffering more than others have, which is, of course, true. Finally, however, God decides that Job, by speaking against God in his suffering, has spoken wrongly, but that in contending against his friends about his innocence before the suffering came, Job has spoken the truth. So the book carries this story ultimately to this

---

[7] Martin Luther, *Luther's Works,* (edited by Theodore G. Tappert, American Edition, Vol. 35 (Philadelphia: Fortress Press, 1960), p. 251.

conclusion: God alone is righteous, and yet one man is more righteous than another, even in the sight of God.

For before Job comes into fear of death, he praises God at the theft of his goods and the death of his children. But when death is in prospect and God withdraws himself, Job's words show what kind of thoughts a man—however holy he may be—holds toward God: he thinks that God is not God, but only a judge and wrathful tyrant, who storms ahead and cares nothing about the goodness of a person's life. This is the finest part of this book. It is understood only by those who also experience and feel what it is to suffer the wrath and judgment of God, and to have his grace hidden. (35:251)

The next quotation is another form of the previous quotation, found in the German "Weimar" edition. This quotation, as well as the two that follow, are taken from "Luther on Job," in the *Concordia Reference Bible, New International Version,* (St. Louis: Concordia, 1989), pages 593-595. The quotations were translated by Robert L. Rosin:

Why Do the Righteous Suffer?

The book of Job deals with this question: Does misfortune come from God, even to righteous people? Job stands firm here and maintains that God torments even the righteous without revealing a reason except that this serves to praise God. Christ testifies to that in John 9:3 concerning the man born blind.

Job's friends oppose that. They babble on at great length, saying that God does not punish a righteous person. If he does, then that person must have sinned. They have such a worldly and human idea

298

about God and his righteousness, as if he were just like men and his justice were like the world's.

However, when Job approaches the anguish of death, he also speaks too much against God. So he sins during his suffering. And yet Job insists that he has not deserved such suffering any more than others have, which is also true. Ultimately God decides that Job did speak unjustly during his suffering when he spoke against God. Yet in the face of suffering, what Job maintained about his innocence (against his friend who presumed he was guilty), Job said rightly.

So this book leads the story finally to this point: God alone is righteous; and yet one person is more righteous than another, also as God sees things. But this is written for our comfort, [telling us] that God even lets his great saints stumble, particularly in adversity. Before Job becomes afraid of death, he praises God at the theft of his goods and the death of his children. But when death stares him in the face and God withdraws, Job's words show what sort of thoughts a person has against God (no matter how holy that person may be). He thinks that God is not God but merely a judge and an angry tyrant who pushes ahead with force and does not ask about anyone's good life. This is the best part of the book. It is understood only by those who also experience and feel what it is to suffer God's anger and judgment and to have his grace be hidden.[8]

---

[8] Martin Luther, *Werke* (Weimar: Boehlau, 1883), *Deutsche Bibel,* Vol. 10/1, pp. 4-6 (editor's translation). See also Martin Luther, *Luther's Works,* Vol. 35, pp. 251-52.

A First Commandment Test

The book of Job wonderfully teaches a lesson and is nearly a one-of-a-kind teacher of a theological example. It has one proposition which runs through the whole book: I am without hope; God is an enemy to me and I to him. . . . It tests the First Commandment: I am in doubt about whether God wants to be compassionate or to do me harm. Why does God plague me and let [my enemies] go their way? Why does he latch on to me, a poor man? Indeed, is my flesh iron, as the text says (Job 6:12)? Then others speak out against this, saying, "You must be a rogue, otherwise this would not happen to you" (Job 4ff.). Job replies, "Ah, is that how you comfort? I know that I do not deserve this" (Job 6). They counter, "You must have done something secretly, otherwise this would not happen to you this way" (Job 8). Then Job says, "Even I have to complain about this. Is our Lord God just? He does not prove it to me" (Job 9).

The Good and Blessed End

Nevertheless, the end is good. It leads to the remission of sins. Normally our Lord God and Job would scold each other, but in the end they are united in the remission of sins. God says, "Do you seek to accuse me?" And Job responds, "It is true that I have spoken too much." But God ends things and says to Job's friends, "You do not speak justly." [God says that] because they should comfort him. So properly, they should first of all lead everything back to the commandment. Then Job replies, "You torment me.

I know what you are. The law does nothing; being pious also does nothing. I see clearly that things happen to godly people just like they happen to evil ones. Therefore I will not feel differently [i.e., become resentful toward God]." This is a great lesson.

The friends do not say to Job, "Even if you have sinned, would you then be afraid?" Rather they say, "If you have sinned, you should make amends." But God concludes this way: "Job ought to pray for you." So God ends things with the remission of sins.... Here is an impressive example of great tribulation and patience...."[9]

The book of Job is a very good book, written not only about and for him, but also for the comfort of all distressed, assaulted, suffering, and afflicted hearts. When the devil and people sharply attack Job and pressure him, he endures it with patience and says, "The name of the Lord be praised" (Job 1:21). But when God begins to be angry with him, Job becomes impatient and annoyed. It galls and hurts him that things go well for the ungodly. The poor Christian is persecuted about this and must suffer. So it is a comfort that God wants to give him such great, magnificent, and eternal things in the life to come. And here God also gives a certain amount of suffering, [allowing] how far and how wide the

[9] Martin Luther, *Werke* (Weimar: Boehlau, 1883-), *Tischreden*, vol. 1, no. 142 (editor's translation).

persecutors can go, but not letting them do all that they would like to do. . . .[10]

Translator's comment: If Job's friends had emphasized the Gospel, they would have told Job not to fear, even if he had sinned. He should trust in God's grace instead. But the friends wrongly advise Job to seek comfort in the Law, telling him to try to make up for whatever he had done. Job rightly rejects that. In citing God's remark, Luther suggests that while Job can be pitied, the ones who really need help are Job's friends with their law-based theology.

---

[10] Martin Luther, *Werke* (Weimar: Boehlau, 1883-), *Tischreden*, vol. 1, no. 475 (editor's translation).

Scripture Index

Genesis
3:15-24 51
3:22-24 52
4:1-16 53
4:12-14 54
6:5-7 54
6:9 29
11:1-9 55
15:3-6 213
22:15-18 215, 216

Deuteronomy
31:8 56
32:4 160
32:18 56
32:22-25 57

1 Samuel
13:14 165

2 Kings
5:1-3 65

Job
1:1,2 ix
1,2 85
1:3 6
1:5 6
1:6 7
1:8 5, 7, 170, 253
1:9 8
1:11 8, 21
1:12 8, 151
1:12; 2:10 151
1:21 9, 20, 39, 301

1:22 9, 40, 49, 79, 204
2:1ff 19
2:3 5, 16, 17, 20, 46, 161, 188, 252, 253
2:4,5 17, 21
2:6 99
2:7,8 17
2:9 17, 22, 43
2:10 18, 20, 39, 40, 79, 151, 204
2:11 18
2:12,13 18
3:23 92
4:1ff 300
4:6 93
4:6-9 83
4:7-9 94
4:8,9 22
4:16,17 94
4:18 94
4:20,21 84
5:13 34
5:17 31, 149, 251
5:17,18 83
5:18 95, 266
5:27 95, 115
6:1ff 300
6:3 97
6:5-7 97
6:8,9 187
6:8-13 97
6:10 98, 187
6:11-13 188
6:12 300
6:14 98
6:21 91

7:5 91, 99
7:17-19 100
7:8 100
7:13 86
7:16 100
7:17-19 100
7:20,21 89
7:21 101
8:1ff 300
8:3-7 83
8:8-10 116
8:11-22 185
8:20 85
9:1ff 300
9:2 85, 118, 125, 126, 185
9:5-13 268
9:14 188
9:14-15 268
9:15 86
9:15-19 188
9:16,17 161
9:17 161
9:19 268
9:20-21 189
9:22 127
9:22-24 160
9:27,28 127
11:2 132
11:2,3 124
11:5,6 84, 116
11:6 132
11:7-11 266
11:12 132
11:13,14,17 267
12:2 86, 118
12:3 133, 185
12:4 133
12:13 134

12:16 134
12:23-25 134
13:5 118
13:8 153
13:12 134
13:13,14 189
13:13,15 268
13:15 190
13:16 190
13:20-22 269
13:24 135
13:26 136
14:3,4 136
14:11,12 190
14:13 136
14:13-15 191
14:15 136
14:16,17 137, 191
14:18,19 191
14:19 137
15:2 149
15:9,10 116
15:10 149
15:32,33 150
16:5 150
16:8 150
16:9 151
16:11 151
16:12 151
16:16,17 152, 192
16:18-21 192
16:22 192
17:1,2 193
17:3 152, 193
17:6,7 193
17:9 154
17:13,14 235
18:19 155
19:2-6 155

19:6 155, 157
19:6-8 194
19:7-11 41
19:10,11 156
19:11 170
19:13-17 91
19:20 91
19:20-22 194
19:21 156
19:22 156
19:23,24 194
19:25 113
19:25,26 236
19:25-27 128, 194
19:28,29 195
19:29 170
20:3 170
20:4,5 116, 171
20:22 171
20:27,29 171
21:13 172
21:14,15 172
21:29 173
21:29,30 120
21:34 121
22:1-11 237
22:5 97, 180
22:21,22 181
22:24,25 181
23:2 183
23:2-4 195
23:3,4 182
23:5-7 196
23:6 183
23:7 183
23:6,7 182
23:8,9 196
23:10 183
23:10-12 196

23:13-16 197
23:16 183
23:17 184
24:1 184
24:12 184
24:25 184
25:6 185
26:2 185
26:2-4 118
26:4 185
26:7-14 270
26:14 186
27:2 204
27:3-6 241
27:5 90, 205
27:6 205
27:7 205
27:19,20 206
28:1-10 35
28:12 206
28:13 207
28:19 207
28:20 207
28:22 207
28:23 207
28:27 207
28:27,28 119
28:28 207
29:2 208
29:2,5 208
29:18 209
29:28 201
30:11 209
30:18-21 210
30:26 210
30:30 91
30:31 210
31:1-3 211
31:6 210

31:33,34 211
31:35 211
31:36 211
31:37 211
31:40 212
32:2 45, 232, 246
32:3 45
32:7,8 117
33:5 248
33:9 246
33:10 246
33:12,13 246
33:14 234
33:15,16 234
33:17 234
33:17,18 244
33:18 234
33:19 234, 251
33:22 235
33:24 236
33:25,26 236
33:27 237
33:27,28 236
33:29-31 237
33:31-33 117
33:32-33 248
34:11 238
34:19 239
35:3 240
35:16 241
36:15 242
36:15-17 245, 249
36:21-16 267
35:16 242
36:22,23 242
36:24 243
37:12,13 54
37:13 243
37:16 243

37:23,24 243
38:1 30, 45
38:2 157
38:4 289
40:2 157
40:5 158
40:8 157
41:10-11 157
42:2,3 31
42:3 158, 168
42:5 30
42:6 30
42:7 31, 205
42:7,8 33, 81, 197
42:7-17 264
42:8 32, 33, 34, 247
42:9 33
42:11 22
42:17 35

Psalms
1:5,6 85
7:3-10 219
7:17 221
73:2-5 122
73:18 122
73:19-20 122
73:21-24 123
73:23,26 282
103:8-10 282
111:7,8 160
116:12-15 65
131:1-3 291

Proverbs
3:11,12 59
3:33-35 121
5:21-23 126

11:15 153

Ecclesiastes
1:13 96
7:15 96, 121

Isaiah
57:1,2 123
64:5-7 218

Jeremiah
4:11 255
9:23,24 168

Lamentations
3:37,38 23

Ezekiel
13,14 28
14:14,20 254
19,20 28

Daniel
9:23 29

Matthew
5:45 67
17:5 214
25:20,21 217
25:21 182
25:31-46 218
26:39,42 214

Mark
9:48 57

Luke
5:8,9 66
6:8-13 98

6:45 278
13:1-5 63

John
8:56 11
9:1-3 62
9:3 297, 298
15:1,2 60
15:2 219
15:5 219
15:9,10 214
15:16 219

Acts
5:1-11 59
5:41 62
14:17 67
15:1ff 11

Romans
1,2 82
1:27 164
2:3,4 164
2:4 66
2:29 86
4:1-3 11
4:1-3,13 215, 216
5:3-5 60
8:36 64

1 Corinthians
3:19 34
11:29-32 58

2 Corinthians
1:3-7 61

Galatians
2:21 213

3:7-9 11
5:6 214, 215
6:8 85

1 Timothy
2:4 57

Hebrews
5:7,8 61
7:2 10
11:4 12, 53
11:7 55
11:9,10 12
11:13-16 13
11:24-26 12
11:39,40 13
12:4-6 59
12:12,13 59

James
1:2-4 60
2:20-24 215, 216
2:26 215
5:10 28
5:11 10, 27, 28,
      50, 249, 254

1 Peter
1:4,6,7 64
4:1,2 60
4:12-14 62
5:8 47

2 Peter
2:5 55

1 John
3:12 53

Revelation
6:15-17 57
22:3 53